EMPOWERING PEOPLE AT WORK

Gower

EMPOWERING PEOPLE AT WORK

NANCY FOY

Published by
Gower Publishing Limited
Gower House
Croft Road
Aldershot
Hampshire GU11 3HR
England

Gower
Old Post Road
Brookfield
Vermont 05036
USA

Nancy Foy Cameron has asserted her right to be identified as the author of this work.

British Library Cataloguing in Publication Data

Foy, Nancy
  Empowering People at Work
  I. Title
  658.3

  ISBN 0–566–07436–2

Library of Congress Cataloging-in-Publication Data

Foy, Nancy.
  Empowering people at work / Nancy Foy.
      p.   cm.
  Includes index.
  ISBN 0–566–07436–2
  1. Self-directed work groups.   2. Management–Employee
participation.   3. Communication in management.   I. Title.
HD88.F68   1993   93–35661
658.4'036–dc20   CIP

Typeset in 10 point Palatino by
Raven Typesetters, Ellesmere Port, South Wirral
and printed in Great Britain at the University Press, Cambridge

For my husband

JOHN C F CAMERON

a fine empowering manager

Contents

Figures

Preface

Who Manages the Empowering?

Managers do, that's who.

Empowering people must *not* mean disempowering managers. People want to be managed. They want to be managed well. They want their leaders to lead them, pointing the way, focusing on priorities, feeding back on how they are doing. There is no room for management abdication in an organisation that is trying to empower its people.

My objective for this book is to share my experience and observations for the benefit of practical managers, coping with real people in real organisations. Chairman Mao once wrote:

> Go to the practical people and learn from them: then synthesise their experience into principles and theories; and then return to the practical people and call upon them to put these principles and methods into practice so as to solve their problems and achieve freedom and happiness.

We need to develop Schumacher's concept of *subsidiarity* in large organisations – the idea that decisions should be made as close to the ground as possible. Real change in large organisations comes from the middle, where people hold the balance between order and freedom. Real managers in the middle who know their own problems can develop practical ways in which to solve them, and those ways can bring development for the people at the bottom. Occasionally, the people at the top recognise what is happening and help it to happen in other parts of the company.

The bedrock on which empowerment rests is information; managers must manage with incomplete information, but opening up listening channels provides managers and their organisations with more and more valid information about what change is possible.

The book is in four parts. The first illustrates how the elements of empowerment work together: performance focus, real teams, visible leadership, and good two-way face-to-face communication. It explores some of the ideas about people and organisations that support empowerment.

Part II shows how to manage empowerment. Empowering has to be part of an organisation's strategy, and there are ways in which it can involve its people in developing the plan. 'Culture change' may be popular, but the culture belongs to its members, just as performance belongs to the performers; managing culture change is a delicate task, if you want to avoid creating cynics and hypocrites. Downsizing and delayering can empower people, or leave them insecure and depressed. Middle managers and supervisors have to be informed and empowered themselves before they can be expected to implement empowering strategies from above. This part concludes with chapters on networks for information and action, listening effectively, keeping team meetings relevant and useful, giving individuals and groups performance feedback, training for empowerment, and using employee surveys as 'tin openers' for change.

Part III presents in-depth case studies of IBM and BT, and examines ways they have developed employee communication to help achieve corporate objectives, including significant downsizing and delayering in the current climate. Whether people in such large organisations are more empowered in today's climate remains to be seen.

Part IV, Resources for Empowering, includes an extensive analysis of communication channels, listed alphabetically for the reader's convenience, a 'pick-and-mix' set of survey questions, and an annotated list of books which I see as milestones along the road to empowerment.

Empowering people is not a nice, soft, fuzzy process. In the best of circumstances, with real top-management commitment and support, it is hard work. If you leave out bits, or cut a few corners, you risk losing your credibility, falling into the chasm of hypocrisy. If you do it right, you're unlikely to be thanked, but you have a better chance to win, and your people have a better chance to do good work.

'Empowering' people is as important today as 'involving' them was in the 1980s, or getting them to 'participate' in the 1970s. Like their predecessors, today's chief executives ('CEOs' in the modern idiom) have a tendency to decree: 'Empower people!', and then demand instant measures of their empowerment – a somewhat dis-empowering way to lay down the law.

The literature on empowering tends to be written by lovely people – but most of them have obviously never had to suffer an imposed budget cut that overnight eliminates all the training a key group has been planning for six months, or a chairman's *ex cathedra* pronouncements that everyone will go on an expensive two-day course to learn to be empowered, just as normal training budgets are cut, and the local dictator has told people stretched to the limit to stop complaining and work harder.

Most of the books I have seen on empowering have buried in them somewhere a Road-to-Damascus sort of experience, the Great Light of Empowerment on the horizon – and a change of behaviour on the part of a supervisor. In a large organization, it is not the poor supervisor who needs exhortation! Most supervisors, like their people, would like to do good work. Very seldom do they get (much less interpret and deliver) clear messages about what 'good work' really is this week, who wants it, and why. Every reorganisation, every pronouncement from too-high, every divergence between what people say, and what they do leaves the supervisor disempowered, and the organisation less manageable as a result.

I have tried to be 'politically correct' with regard to gender, but many years as a minority woman in the men's corridors of power may have caused a slip here or there. If I write 'he' the reader should fill in 'he or she'. In the UK women account for only 3 per cent of senior management, and 9 per cent of all management, yet women make up about half the workforce, and even more are going out to work now. Women employees can be more flexible, better at team working, they can manage change and network more effectively. The top teams that do not contain women are depriving themselves of skills they will need to manage modern organisations.

May I say to managers what Doctor Spock once said to mums: if the advice of experts, including me, conflicts with your own instincts, trust your instincts. You are the one with the best information.

I do not believe that an ideal organisation exists, which is full of ideal teams led by ideal managers. But the real world is interesting enough, and every large organisation I have ever encountered had plenty of room to move towards becoming manageable. I hope this book helps real managers help it happen.

Nancy Foy

Acknowledgements

During the exhilarating 1970s I was able to learn about IBM and Volvo in some depth. Pehr Gyllenhammar and Tom Watson Jr are still important models of management for me.

Several years ago Colin Minton and I spent a few days pooling our experiences, with a view to writing a book on employee 'involvement'. Material we generated then has fed into this book, just as the 1980s interest in involvement was itself a precursor to the 1990s interest in empowerment.

I had a number of managers in my mind's ear at various times as I wrote about empowering. Among them were Harry Archibald, Cyril Bleasdale, Tim Brett, Julia Colclough, David Cruikshank, Alastair Duff, Paul Duffin, Billy Easton, Jack Fallow, Mac Farquhar, Bill Furness, Eileen Gill, Chris Greene, Bob Heasman, Ruth Kirkman, David Kogan, Simon Lane, Russell Lee, Verity Marshall, Norman McCandlish, John McClelland, David McCracken, John McLachlan, Vernon Murphy, Alan Penman, Mandy Pritchett, Jean Ramsay, David Roberts, Ann Shor, John Simpson, Richard Spoors, John Stokdyk, Peter Summerhayes, the late Joan Sweeney, Ronnie Telford, Max Tighe, Jan Walsh, John Wesley.

Authors always thank their publishers, but Malcolm Stern, Gower's Editorial Director, deserves particularly heartfelt recognition for his support and encouragement, not just now, but over the 20 years we have been roaming the same patch of turf. I appreciate his depth of understanding, and his warmth and tact have made this book a happy experience.

My sister Jennie Burton coaxed me into WordPerfect and expanded my definition of 'empowering'. Finally, let me turn the tables on those who thank their wives for typing and cooking. My husband John has listened when I needed him to, and not listened when I didn't; he has been a splendid critic and mentor; and sometimes at the expense of his own research he has kept the home-fires burning through a succession of blizzards that allowed me to finish the book on time.

Nancy Foy
Killiecrankie
July 1993

Part I

The Empowering Organisation

When people in an organisation are empowered, you can walk in the door and feel the difference. People look you straight in the eye. They show a proactive, outgoing curiosity. You sense their confidence; it emanates from individuals, but it is supported by teams, by managers they respect, and by the empowering organisation itself.

This section looks at this overall model for practical empowering: a focus on performance, real teams, visible leadership, and good communication. Fitting these pieces together so that they mesh seamlessly is the art of empowering.

The empowering organisation, the one that is good for its members, is not necessarily a company. Think of a fine, confident school; think of a good hospital; think of a prizewinning theatre company. The same principles are operating, because people are people, however they invest their lives. They deserve to invest them in wholesome, healthy organisations.

1

Empowered People

Organisations are not empowered, people are. Organisations can give power, or take it away. The empowering organisation puts the spotlight on winning, on giving people opportunities to perform to their maximum effectiveness.

Empowered people need to give and receive many kinds of information, to know how well they are performing and what is expected of them. The empowering organisation, in turn, needs to listen, to find out what prevents peak performance, and how it can be improved. People need to know what is going on in the organisation, and how their work dovetails with others.

The empowering organisation actually *wants* to tap people's knowledge and experience. Therefore, as a wise investment, it must develop people. That means it must develop their teams, too. Development for the managers, like development for individuals, comes from many opportunities to tackle new challenges, learning to co-operate with others, the development of the organisation, in turn, stems from the development of the individuals, teams and managers.

The means by which the empowering organisation achieves performance, communication and development is leadership. When confident leaders can support confident teams of empowered individuals, everyone wins.

The people who know a job best are those who do it. Those people want to do good work. Most of them spend at least eight hours a day, more than half their waking hours, at work. They deserve the chance to do good work. Organisations that want success simply find ways to let them.

What is Empowerment?

'What's the difference between "empowerment" and "delegation"?' a colleague asked. A picture of a wispy 12-year-old girl popped into my head.

'If you give your daughter money to buy a pair of jeans, that's delegation,' I suggested. 'If you give her a clothes allowance she can spend as she chooses, that's empowerment.'

Empowerment is not quite that simple, but the clothes allowance analogy is a useful starting-point. When 12-year-old Ann demanded a clothes allowance, she then went out and spent it on all sorts of things that in my view were not very useful. I could have corrected her, or stopped her allowance – or watched as she learned; for several years I had to give her boring presents like socks and knickers for birthday, Christmas, Easter, and any other pretext, until she learned to fine-tune her budget for herself. Empowerment is not an overnight process.

A cluster of trainers in a large company with advanced personnel policies were discussing their empowerment workshops with enthusiasm. 'The troops here want to become empowered,' they said. 'They're telling us: "Give me the opportunity to do this!" It's not like a campaign where you have to make them want something, like quality. It's quite natural for them. The problem is with their managers, who have trouble letting go, or feel that empowering their people might take away some of their own power.'

In an advanced company, where they are already well informed and involved, employees relish a chance to put relationships with their managers on a more adult-to-adult basis.

In an organisation where people have had less involvement and have less confidence in themselves and their managers, the initial reaction may be to shy away from empowering opportunities. 'It's just a job; I don't want the responsibility.' Some 12-year-olds manage to obtain more clothes by cajoling and nagging than they might with a clothes allowance. The parent–child model involves certain comforts.

Empowerment is simply gaining the power to make your voice heard, to contribute to plans and decisions that affect you, to use your expertise at the work to improve your performance – and with it the performance of your whole organisation.

The Hamstrung Organisation

People are too seldom empowered in large organisations. Why is this? Because normal people in normal organisations take small disempowering steps, or fail to take empowering steps, in normal situations. Other normal people observe, and learn what should and should not be done if they want to get ahead, or survive. Once they evolve a set of beliefs about the organisation, it takes on a life of its own and hardens into a shell of 'culture'.

What is the opposite of the empowering organisation? How about 'the hamstrung organisation', meaning thwarted, impeded or made inefficient? Hogwash! Organisations should not thwart or impede people, and people should not thwart or impede organisations. They need each other, and both need to be efficient.

Today we have many organisations embarked on 'empowering' – a tacit recognition that their people have become disempowered. The larger the organisation, the more difficult the road to empowerment. Most people, however, work in normal large organisations, and most people feel hamstrung, crippled in their desire to do good work.

Hamstrung People

The sum in an organisation is supposed to be greater than the parts. For more than 80 years IBM developed the highly integrated structure that was able to cover every aspect of the changing market for office machinery. Mere typewriter salesmen were consigned to places 'below the salt', while the élite IBMers sold monolithic computers to large corporate customers. Now, with nimble little competitors on every side selling personal computers as if they were hi-fi sets, IBM-watchers are wondering out loud whether the company can break itself up fast enough to survive in new and different market-places. Empowering individual IBMers is becoming a strategic imperative, and difficult for a company whose role with employees has always been that of the good parent.

Most organisations actually waste much of the capability of the people who have invested themselves there. General Motors or Henry Ford were not the only ones to develop the 'efficient' model in which everything is tucked into tidy boxes in an orderly hierarchy. Although Frederick Winslow Taylor is often given credit for their stopwatch-based 'scientific management', he certainly did not invent hierarchy; hierarchy is how the Roman

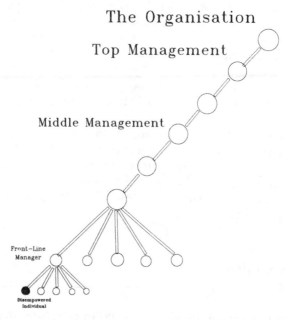

Figure 1.1 The 'Them' Model

legions won, and how the Catholic Church organised itself. It works when everybody knows the clear-cut, unchanging objective.

In what I call the 'Them' model, it is them, up there, who set the procedures and rules, who decide what is to be done and how. They want only my hands or back, not my brain. They only expect us and me to do our little well-specified bit, and keep doing it dependably. If they don't treat me well enough, I can get bloody-minded, along with my colleagues, and thwart them. There is not a great deal I can do to change things, so I don't bother – and I don't bother working very hard either. As Figure 1.1 shows, the organisation is writ large, and the individual writ small. Power is up there, helplessness is down here. So be it. It's just a job.

What a waste! John Garnett, larger-than-life leader of the Industrial Society for many years, used to preach to the leaders of large organisations: 'With every pair of hands, you get a free brain.'

I should like to help furnish a world where people encounter fewer cultural, bureaucratic, and management hurdles, where they own themselves, where they are able to contribute their knowledge and experience.

In empowering organisations, people know what the organisation expects from them, and how well they are meeting their targets. More than that, in the ultimate empowering, they are able to help develop the objectives, and their experience feeds into the development of credible strategies. That kind of organisation will be good for its members, and they will be good for the organisation.

The 'Me' Model

To achieve this admirable (but all too rare) way of working, the organisation needs to respect what the individual can offer it. The empowered person feels at the centre, part of a team that can achieve. The team's own leader, and other leaders, co-ordinate and communicate to eliminate problems and help the individual and team do good work. Once that empowered individual knows what the organisation needs, and why; top management becomes relatively less important than the chance to deliver good performance – for one's own satisfaction, and recognition from one's team and leader. We might call this the 'Me' model, (see Figure 1.2).

The empowered individual wants to (and is able to) deliver performance. And that is what the organisation wants. The empowered individual can also help develop the organisation, to influence its processes and strategies, just as the organisation can help develop the individual, the team, and the managers. Mutual development is the key to meeting change.

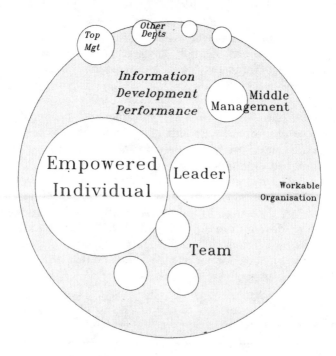

Figure 1.2 The 'Me' Model

The empowered individual has information that the organisation needs, just as the organisation has information that the individual needs. Performance is the primary focus for information, but every other aspect of working life is important for full consonance between 'me' and 'them', to the benefit of both.

In this model, the empowering leader informs, develops, and helps people to perform – and to deliver their performance, information and development for the organisation. The front-line manager, empowering individuals, determines the success of the strategies set by well-informed higher management, and the ability of the team to set and meet wholesome objectives.

On Beyond Taylor

Toyota and General Motors combined forces to turn Frederick Taylor's principles upside down – with interesting results.[1] For ten years they worked together to turn one of the worst GM factories, in Fremont, California, into a model of high performance.

GM closed Fremont in 1982 after four wildcat strikes; it had always been a problem plant, with high drug and alcohol abuse, astronomical absenteeism, abysmal productivity and low morale. When Toyota suggested a joint project, to see whether Japanese management techniques would work with American workers, GM offered Fremont.

Though the Japanese would have preferred a non-union plant, GM insisted they retain the UAW branch, to preserve peace in other GM locations. So they opened in 1984, with the union, and 85 per cent of the 2200 shop floor people came from the previous GM workforce. They called the new business New United Motor Manufacturing Inc (NUMMI).

Paul Adler, a professor at the University of Southern California, spent two years studying NUMMI. Reporting in the November–December 1992 *Harvard Business Review*, he described an amazing turnaround, mainly attributed to competition between small teams, good leadership, and giving people the tools to improve their own performance.

Toyota's first step was to convince the workers they were the key to the factory's success. Everyone received training and, after years of job worries, a promise of no lay-offs. Management began to earn some trust.

In the GM era Fremont had 80 white-coated industrial

engineers who set the standards with their stopwatches and clipboards, while supervisors tried to exhort their people to meet the imposed norms. The workforce had no say in the matter, except passive resistance. Under Toyota, the workers were divided into 350 teams of 5–7 plus a leader. Everyone learned Taylor's techniques and was given a stopwatch, so team members could analyse their own jobs, and each others', to improve performance, they naturally learned to do all the jobs in the team this way. Because there were similar teams on the other shifts, they had natural comparisons: as soon as one team made an improvement, the others rushed to learn how they did it, then to better it.

Everything is still standardised at NUMMI, but the people on the floor have some power to improve the standards themselves now. That is empowerment. Instead of the frustration of empty exhortation, team leaders have the reward of visibly improving performance. That is empowerment. Instead of futile chasing, monitoring, counting, arguing and nagging, the white-collar workers have well-defined jobs to support the shop-floor. That is another form of empowerment.

Productivity at NUMMI is more than twice what it was in GM's day, and fast approaching the levels the Japanese achieve with their own workers in Japan. Quality has soared. Drugs, alcohol and absenteeism have almost disappeared. Toyota is so pleased with the results of the project that it has added another assembly line and taken on more staff.

Total empowerment, nevertheless, is a fairy story, and this book is about the real world. But if empowering people even with Taylor's tools can more than double their performance, empowerment is worth implementing.

Note

1. 'Return of the stopwatch', *The Economist*, 23 January 1993.

2

Focus on Performance

People want to do good work. The empowering organisation helps them, the hamstrung organisation hinders them.

The difference between the two is often subtle: a person can be a winner in an empowering organisation, and the same person doing the same things can be a loser in a hamstrung organisation. One key factor that can make the difference is the organisation's focus on performance.

For every group in every organisation, there are customers. This is one of the basic concepts in quality, and improving customer links is a fine approach to performance. Part of the art of management is helping people learn more about who their customers are, and what they want.

People Want to Do Good Work

In the empowering organisation, everyone understands what 'good work' is. Individually, in groups, in functions, they know what is expected of them, and the organisation in turn knows what they can deliver.

In the hamstrung organisation, planners working in the dark

leave gaps between their own expectations and those of the people who have to carry out the plans. If the plan is too slack, people don't bother, while if it is too stringent then it becomes impossible, so they still don't bother.

The difference between empowered and hamstrung is an intertwined combination of information and motivation. The better the information people have, the more motivated they can be, and the better the information they give their management, the more unified and motivated the organisation can be.

In the empowering organisation, people know what their bosses expect, but they also understand what their customers see as good work. Most organisations, including some with expensive TQM programmes, have better machinery for finding out what external customers expect than they do for exploring the needs of internal customers. Yet the best results frequently come from responding better to in-house customer needs.

A group is often encouraged to see higher-ups as customers, at the expense of other groups or departments who depend on their outputs. Colin Minton[1] calls this 'inward-upward management'. An organisation that really values performance will ultimately have to put a premium on 'downward–outward managers', because their people are able to deliver.

Some Useful Old Models

Today's concept of empowerment is based on some well-established ideas about what makes people tick, as individuals and in groups. When I began trying to help organisations focus on performance, I found myself harking back to early models of management that still are valid for empowering organisations.

Role v Task

I often found myself drawing circles on blackboards or flipcharts, and thinking fondly of Alistair Mant,[2] who first showed me that it was the difference between role and task that caused most family squabbles.

The question of whose job it is to wash the dishes inevitably

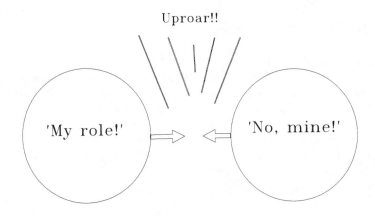

Figure 2.1 The Role Model

leads to conflict, hasty words, long silences. That is a role question.

If, instead, the question is 'Will we have time to wash the dishes before we go to the pub?' the focus on task leads instead to co-operation with shared activity and conversation. So it is in working groups. As soon as you start considering roles you are embroiled in office politics; who is encroaching on whose patch. You are draining energy away from the place where people want it – on doing that good work, on performing.

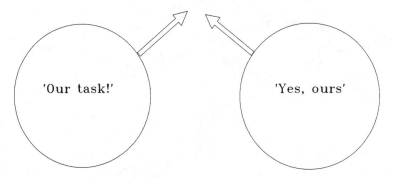

Figure 2.2 The Task Model

Management by Objectives

John Humble would want Peter Drucker to have the credit for MBO, but it was Humble's efforts to spread the concept that put the term into everyday use. For the past 25 years at least, organisations have set objectives and measured how well people met them. I recall one executive, now well into retirement, who used to say, 'Yeah, we have MBO here. I decide people's objectives and kick ass until they deliver.' Nobody had much of a hand in setting their own objectives – but on the other hand, they certainly knew what he expected of them.

Herzberg's Hygiene

Back in the same effervescent period of change – late 'sixties and early 'seventies – Fred Herzberg[3] offered a turning-point for many of us when he distinguished between 'hygiene factors' and 'motivators'. The hygiene factors kept people from being unhappy; it was the motivators that excited them. Herzberg had an elaborate model and some very sensible ways of dealing with

Hygiene Factors	Motivators
Pay	*Fun*
Environment	*Achievement*
Not losing	*Winning!*
Pension	*Avoiding tax*
etc.	*etc.*
etc.	*etc.*

Figure 2.3 Hygiene Factors and Motivators

people once managers saw the difference between hygiene factors and motivators.

It surprised me then to realise that pay was not a motivator but a hygiene factor. Thinking about it now, however, how much more often do you hear people grumbling about something unfair with respect to pay, and how seldom does anyone say: 'Getting my salary really turns me on.'

Money only becomes a motivator when it's a sign you're winning, which leads to Foy's corollary to Herzberg's and everyone else's laws:

Winning is fun. Not-losing is not-fun.

Maslow's Hierarchy

This is the most pervasive model of all. When I first learned about Maslow's work,[4] back in the 'fifties, it was an exciting new idea – that people had a hierarchy of needs. We thought then that you could only move on from one need to the next when the first had been fulfilled. Our names for the needs were a little different (as Figure 2.4 shows). Today we talk about 'self-esteem'.

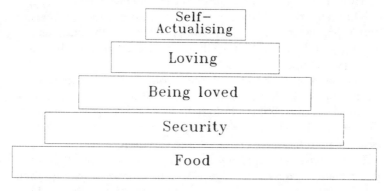

Figure 2.4 Maslow's Hierarchy of Needs

As time went on we began to view Maslow more flexibly. In the old days we assumed it was only Bertrand Russell who was confident enough to be self-actualising. Nowadays most people on the shop floor seem to be bouncing between security and self-actualisation – often several times in a single day. The model is still useful to me, because it highlights the creative need that is built into people.

The Empowered Group

Let us consider a hypothetical meeting of a group, one of many inside an empowering organisation. Like everyone else, its members like to keep an eye on whether they're winning or not. Their counterparts in the hamstrung organisation can only measure (and improve on) the number of tea breaks they award themselves. In the empowered group, they have more interesting measures.

The team leader starts with parish notices and some one-line summaries from a 'core brief' that comes down regularly from on high. The company is giving groups £5 per employee for their Christmas celebrations, and organising coaches to take people home after parties. The organisation has met its targets for the quarter, and exceeded them by 5 per cent on several counts.

'How does that fit with our own performance?' he asks.

'Our deliveries to Final Assembly are running about 3 per cent better than target,' says one member. 'They like the new casings we suggested, and we'll have those in work by next week, which will ease the old bottleneck.'

Another member reports on the chronic Stores problem. 'With a lot of nagging we've cut the number of outstanding items by about 10 per cent, but it would help if you'd ask the boss to invite the Stores Manager and maybe the foreman to attend his next management meeting to discuss the situation.'

They discuss not only the inputs and outputs, but their own performance – timekeeping, how well flexitime is working – then get down to the serious business of what they want to do for a Christmas celebration. The meeting takes about half an hour, and by the time it is finished they feel that a couple of problems have been solved. The keeper of the charts goes out with his magic markers to record their chosen performance indicators on the large wall chart for all to see, while the supervisor jots down a few notes for his file, and a couple more to let his boss know the group's performance for the period.

One major difference between this empowered group and a hamstrung group is that *the group itself decided what measures were most appropriate*. At first they had set one or two measures that were impracticable, and involved more effort than they were worth. Then there was that Stores item – something they could not control without involving managers higher up. They had finally put it at the end of the list as 'Stores Nagging: number of orders unfilled' – and the people in Stores at least started explaining *why* things were out of stock.

It might be tempting for a manager to say, 'I could have saved you all that trouble. I knew you couldn't make much headway with Stores.' That 'I told you so' might be fun for him, – but it is a downright demotivator for the group itself.

The empowering manager simply smiles at the supervisor and says, 'Thank you! That's quite a breakthrough about the new casings. Sounds as if you're building good relationships there.' The next morning, walking by the group's chart-board, he tells a couple of members how pleased he is at the 3 per cent over-target deliveries. And, at the group's behest, he spends more time with the Stores Manager trying to understand the reasons for the bottlenecks.

If Stores indeed needs some new systems or investment, the empowering manager may be an ally of the Stores Manager, on behalf of the group that needs better deliveries. If the problems in Stores can be alleviated by simpler means (like showing Stores what their customers value, and how performance might be measured), his interested support is the most useful stance for a potential in-house consultant.

Eaton, an American company, influenced the thinking of Nissan when they were setting up their UK factory, according to Peter Wickens.[5] Eaton's published philosophy statement begins:

> Eaton understands that the success of the company depends, ultimately, on the performance of its employees. Sustained high performance is most likely when there is a high level of individual commitment to the goals of their organisation.

Eaton's principles focus on mutual trust, mutual respect, and the individual freedom necessary for exceptionally high employee performance – what would certainly be called principles for empowering. Wickens lists the key points of the Eaton philosophy:

- Focus on the positive behaviour of employees.
- Encourage employee involvement in decisions.
- Communicate with employees in a timely and candid way, with emphasis on face-to-face communications.
- Compensate employees competitively under systems which reward excellence.
- Provide training for organisational/individual success.
- Maintain effective performance appraisal systems.
- Emphasise promotion from within throughout the company.
- Select managers and supervisors who demonstrate an appropriate blend of human relations skills and technical competence.

Building on these principles, Eaton set up small groups of operators and supervisors and asked them to redesign plant layouts, cut inventories, and improve lead times. They achieved significant, measurable improvements – lead time is measured in days rather than weeks, and inventories were more than halved.

Nissan's planning was also influenced by Robertson and Smith's[6] practical work, building on Herzberg. This included factors that were important in developing commitment, including:

- Employees should understand the link between effort and performance.
- Employees should have the competence and confidence to translate effort into performance.
- Organisation and job changes should be introduced through consultation and discussion.
- Control systems should be introduced only when necessary.
- Performance should be expressed in terms of hard but attainable goals.
- Employees should participate in setting these goals.
- Feedback should be regular, informative and easy to interpret.
- People should be praised for good performance.

Modern Models

'Customer Care' models have been around for a few years. Now it's becoming clear that awareness of the customer – and being able to achieve performance in line with his needs – is at the root of successful quality programmes. Let us look more closely at the most popular quality model: Total Quality Management.

TQM – Tangible Results for Success

In 1992 the A. T. Kearney management consultancy conducted a survey of more than a hundred organisations that claimed to practise Total Quality Management. According to principal consultant Malcolm Hillyard, half of them did not measure performance. Of the 50 per cent who did, 20 per cent achieved improvements over 12 months, while the other 30 per cent reported no improvements. Hillyard concluded that the few who succeeded combined high employee empowerment with high goal alignment. The successful programmes showed common characteristics:

- tangible results;
- performance measurement;
- benchmarking;
- customer focus;
- top management commitment;
- empowered teams;
- they included 'support activities'.

In other words: *What gets measured, gets done.* In other words, 'The two things that get done are what I want to do, and what the boss asks about.' Hillyard noted that the failed programmes also shared some characteristics:

- They underestimated the commitment and resources TQM would demand.
- Top management said it was committed, but did not show active involvement.
- They made culture-change the focus, and tried to obtain

performance improvement as a by-product (rather than vice versa).

- They had no have clear performance objectives or measures.
- Internal communications were poor.
- They laid great stress on training.
- They had too many teams.
- They were poorly integrated, and had no 'leading edge'.
- They could not show early benefits.

Big Models, Big Ballyhoo

There are other big models that show similar patterns (and most winning models are remarkably similar in their basic demands: top-management commitment, empowered front-line management, good teams, clear objectives, early wins, good monitoring).

Though I speak as a consultant, I would advocate caution concerning most big models touted by consultancies, unless they are certain they have the prerequisites just listed. These big models (including most of the un-winning TQM programmes) usually have common features:

- They are projected from outside.
- They are highly publicised.
- They make many promises.
- They are based on top-down inspirational training cascade (a consultant's charter to coin money).
- They culminate (eventually) in sheep-dip training for the masses.
- They have minuscule monitoring machinery (eg the consultant coming back regularly).
- They demand a great deal of lip service.

It is much better to get your head down and start measuring performance, and letting people know what the tangible results are that you would view as 'winning'.

Foy's Inverted Triangle

This 'model' starts with the traditional triangle, with planners and strategists at the top, divided by an often impregnable wall from the doers, who labour on in the dark down below (or 'win' by awarding themselves all those tea breaks). Most people working inside large organisations, even the most benign and forward-looking organisations, would recognise this model. It is occasionally called the 'mushroom model' 'Keep us in the dark and every now and then open the door and shovel in manure.'

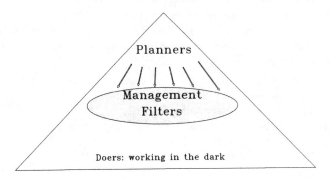

Figure 2.5 Top-down Management

Look what happens, however, if you invert the pyramid:

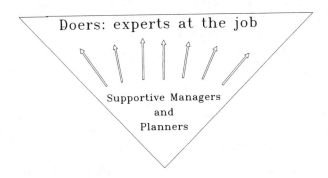

Figure 2.6 The Inverted Triangle

This model, derived in part from an employee's view of Tom Farmer's successful Kwik-Fit formula, shows how important good, open communication is as the first step to empowering people.

Benefits of Communicating Performance

Communicating performance – up, down, and across an organisation, – is just as important as achieving performance. Only through communication can each group's performance ultimately be dovetailed with others so the whole becomes greater than the parts. Synergy depends on communication.

When the task is at the core of everything, and performance can be achieved and communicated, a number of benefits come to the organisation:

- empowered supervisors;
- relevant two-way communication;
- better management information;
- employees able to achieve.

What more could anyone ask?

Notes

1. Colin Minton is a management consultant based in Tewin, Herts. He has been a trade union official, a key manager at the Industrial Society, and right-hand man to Robert Maxwell – not all at once, I hasten to add.

2. Alistair Mant is author of the famous Mant Report, 1970, that first identified the importance of the neglected 'backbone manager'.

3. Fred Herzberg, who did the early work on motivators and hygiene factors, was a famous and peripatetic American management consultant.

4. Abraham Maslow, 1908–70, American psychology expert, worked in existential and humanistic psychology. Best known for his concept of 'self-actualising'.

5. Peter Wickens is Personnel Director at Nissan, and author of *The Road to Nissan* (Basingstoke: Macmillan, 1987).

6. Ian Robertson and M. Smith (1985), *Motivation and Job Design*, London: IPM.

3

Real Teams

What is the sound of one hand clapping? Fine performance comes from fine teams. In empowering people, the sum is greater than the parts – that is 'synergy'. It is also the financial rationale for investing in good teamwork.

'Teamwork' is necessary beyond the confines of the basic team, too. I recall a large computer manufacturer, steeped in the tradition of the industry. The boffins were clever fellows, individualists who would stay up all night, then arrive at the office with abstruse but elegant logic equations that described a new computer. Those scribbles would go to a 'designer' who drew elegant boxes around the logic equations.

Eventually, after a certain amount of healthy competition between designs, a sheaf of blueprints would be passed over the wall to manufacturing, where several people would scratch their heads, tell each other that if they wanted to get somewhere (like to the market-place) they would never have started from here – and get on with making it, somehow. Meanwhile the advertisements would go out, claiming magnificent breakthroughs that few believed.

Things have changed – and that computer company went out of business a long time ago. Today, even the most traditional manufacturer realises you have to have some kind of manufacturing involvement at the design stage if you want something to be makeable.

Competition and Collaboration

A modern phenomenon which ignores this understanding is the bureaucratic obsession with 'compulsory competitive tendering'. All too often, concentration on 'competition' disregards the need for designs to be developed in close co-operation with manufacturing. As a result, the bureaucrats indulge in endless over-specification, regardless of the tenderers' capabilities. The end result costs us far more than would cross-functional collaboration (which the bureaucrats see as 'collusion').

The NUMMI example in Chapter 1 and the BT case in Chapter 19 remind us that competition works best the closer it is to home. Individual managers will work hard to outdo each other on league tables within a single department. Little teams compete to improve performance when they can see other little teams pulling ahead on the same measurements. I doubt that privatising British Rail will give me much better service when main lines are competing for investment. The West still has not even begun to approach the Japanese in using competition and collaboration among teams to develop better products, faster.

Why Don't Cross-functional Teams Work?

At the product development frontier, companies spend fortunes trying to emulate the Japanese with their 'cross-functional teams'. Steven Wheelwright and Kim Clark, both professors at the Harvard Business School (HBS), studied American and Japanese teams, and suggested several reasons why the Western teams don't work as well.[1]

Top Management Commitment

Mixed teams usually threaten someone's 'patch of turf'. Senior managers in the more ambivalent Western hierarchies are better able to resist team demands for use of their resources and without broad support throughout the company, the team doesn't amass enough power to attract and hold the right people and resources.

Cohesion

Lacking the resources they need, these 'lightweight' teams try to fill the gaps by creating outside advisers and satellite teams. This is both inefficient and ineffective. In the car industry, for example, the professors noted the Americans needed 1500 people for their product development teams, compared with just 250 in Japan – where better designs are generated sooner as a result.

Focus

The tighter-knit Japanese 'heavyweight' teams are led by senior managers, have access to the best people, share a clear mission, and own the whole project. The HBS professors note that this kind of 'ownership' encourages responsibility and commitment, which in turn help the team to concentrate on the goal. They mention Hewlett-Packard and Motorola as Western firms that have mastered the use of heavyweight cross-functional teams.

These teams are at the large end (and the sharp end) of the spectrum, but the same principles apply to normal work teams. The team that feels ownership, that has the resources it needs, that enjoys blessings from above, will do better than the one that is fragmented, ambivalent, badly led and under informed.

The Belbin[2] Acid Test

There are more subtle factors than focus at work, too. A person can be a winner in one setting and a loser in another? Why? Whatever the leadership situation, when the mix is right people work better. The sum can, indeed, be greater than the parts.

Dr Meredith Belbin, at Cambridge's Industrial Training Research Unit, has worked for many years to develop a profile of the membership of an effective team. In studying syndicates working at the Henley management programme, he found that some worked better than others. The effective teams covered a number of different roles. (Other experts have suggested slightly different numbers and groupings: Dave Francis translates Belbin's eight roles to ten, and I have changed some of Belbin's role names for easier understanding, but I think Belbin deserves homage for discovering and delineating the mix that works.)

The Belbin approach differs from navel-examining psychology because it is aimed towards using individual strengths to strengthen the team. People (being human) tend to like others who are similar to themselves. It sometimes it takes extra energy to force the people choosing team members to scan the mix of people already there and fill the gaps, instead of selecting more of the same, 'everyone will get on well together'. This work taught me to respect differentness. It can do the same for managers choosing or using teams.

Belbin's work also absolves everyone of guilt: you cannot be all things to all people, you cannot fill every role yourself. Superman is a myth, and has no place in an effective team!

The following 'Team Role Inventory' is adapted slightly from my earlier book[3], and is based on a simplified self-scoring test that takes about ten minutes. The important thing is for team members to share their scores, and negotiate among themselves to fill the missing roles.

Every team needs every one of the roles Belbin identified. Even three people have to perform all eight roles among them if they are to succeed at doing a task together. Most people are fairly comfortable with at least two or three of the roles, though most of us would be able to identify ourselves with one of them in particular. Similarly, most people would be fairly uncomfortable with several of the roles.

Thus there can be no 'wrong' answers. Problems only arise if, within a group, roles remain unfilled – there is no one able or interested in dotting 'i's and crossing 't's, say, or no one to move the team from discussion to action.

Nobody can score higher than anyone else – each section contains 10 points, for a grand total of 70. Everyone achieves 70 points, but the way they are apportioned shows who fills which role in the team.

Team Role Inventory

Below are sets of statements describing attitudes and personal preferences. Each statement has eight choices. You have ten points to apportion among them. The more strongly you feel that a particular response fits you, the higher the number of points you give it. As long as they add up to 10 per statement and thus 70 total, all scores here are 'good'.

1. When involved in a project with other people:
f.   — I can be relied on to see that the work we need to do is organised.
h.   — I detect slips and omissions that others fail to notice.
b.   — I react strongly when meetings look like losing track of the main objective.
d   — I produce original suggestions.
e.   — I analyse other people's ideas objectively for their merits and their flaws.
c.   — I am keen to find out the latest ideas and developments.
a.   — I have an aptitude for organising people.
g.   — I am always ready to support good suggestions that help to resolve a problem.

2. In seeking satisfaction through my work:
b.   — I like to have a strong influence on decisions.
h.   — I am most comfortable when my work requires a high degree of concentration and attention.
g.   — I am concerned to help colleagues with their problems.
e.   — I like to discriminate between alternatives.
d.   — I tend to have a creative approach to problem-solving.
a.   — I enjoy reconciling different points of view.
f.   — I am more interested in practicalities than in new ideas.
c.   — I particularly enjoy exploring different views and techniques.

3. When the team is trying to solve a particularly complex problem:
h.   — I keep a watchful eye on areas where difficulties may arise.
c.   — I explore ideas that may have a wider application than to the immediate task.

e. —I like to weigh up and thoroughly evaluate a range of suggestions before choosing.
a. —I can co-ordinate and productively use other people's abilities and talents.
f. —I maintain a steady, systematic approach, whatever the pressures.
d. —I often produce a new approach to a continuing problem.
b. —I am ready to make my personal views known, in a forceful way if necessary.
g. —I am ready to help wherever I can.

4. In carrying out my day-to-day work:
f. —I am keen to see that there is nothing vague about my task and objectives.
b. —I am not reluctant to emphasise my own point of view at meetings.
a. —I can work with all sorts of people, provided they have something worthwhile to contribute.
c. —I make a point of following up interesting ideas and people.
e. —I can usually find the argument to refute unsound propositions.
d. —I tend to see patterns where others would see items as unconnected.
h. —Being busy gives me real satisfaction.
g. —I am interested in getting to know people better.

5. If I am suddenly given a difficult task with limited time and unfamiliar people:
d. —I often find my imagination frustrated by working in a group.
a. —My personal skills are particularly appropriate to achieving agreement in the group.
e. —My feelings seldom interfere with my judgement.
f. —I strive to build up an effective structure.
g. —I can work with people who vary widely in their personal qualities and outlook.
b. —I feel it is sometimes worth incurring some temporary unpopularity to succeed in getting one's views across in a group.
c. —I usually know the person whose specialist knowledge is particularly apt.

h. — I seem to develop a natural sense of urgency.

6. When suddenly asked to consider a new project:

c. — I start to look around for possible ideas and openings.

h. — I am concerned to finish and perfect current work before I start.

e. — I approach the problem in a carefully analytical way.

b. — I am able to assert myself to involve other people if necessary.

d. — I am able to take an independent and innovative look at most situations.

a. — I am happy to take the lead when action is required.

g. — I can respond positively to my colleagues and their initiatives.

f. — I find it hard to give of my best in a job where the goals are not clearly defined.

7. In contributing to group projects, in general:

f. — I think I have a talent for sorting out the concrete steps that need to be taken, given a broad brief.

e. — My considered judgement may take time, but it is usually near the mark.

c. — A broad range of personal contacts is important to my style of working.

h. — I have an eye for getting the details right.

b. — I try to make my mark in group meetings.

d. — I can see how ideas and techniques can be used in new relationships and situations.

a. — I can see both sides of a problem and take a decision acceptable to all.

g. — I get on well with others and work hard for the team.

Now add the scores for each letter, and put the totals in the boxes below

a	b	c	d	e	f	g	h

Figure 3.1 Team Role Inventory Scores Matrix

The following are the descriptions that go with the letters above. See if they fit your own perceptions.

a. *The Chairman* This is the co-ordinator (not the boss). He or she likes organising people, mapping their strengths, using them productively. This is the person who engineers consent and consensus, developing agreement among different interests. The chairman commands respect and inspires enthusiasm, talks and listens well, and has a sense of discipline, focus, timing and balance. The chairman is not necessarily the most intelligent or most creative member of the team.

b. *The Shaper* This is the outgoing, forceful task-leader type who likes to make a mark in meetings, to influence group decisions. He or she will risk being unpopular to get ideas across. The shaper concentrates on setting objectives and priorities, and making sure the discussion and action take on the right shape or pattern. The shaper's drive and self-confidence may carry a hint of intolerance or impatience with vague or fuzzy people or ideas. This is the one exception to Belbin's rule that you need all roles in a team. A team does *not* need both a chairman and a shaper – they often work against each other.

c. *The Contacts Man* (or woman – Belbin calls this role 'The Resource Investigator'). This is the sociable, relaxed 'butterfly', flitting around the boundaries, looking further afield than the immediate task, bringing in outside ideas, developments, and phone numbers. The butterfly works by personal networks and contacts, likes new ideas and techniques, and can usually find the right specialist to help at a moment's notice. He or she works well on the phone, probably has an outgoing personality, is willing to see possibilities in anything new. The curiosity asset may be accompanied by over-enthusiasm, or a lack of follow up.

d. *The Ideas Man* (or woman – Belbin calls this role 'The Plant'). This is the innovator, the most original, independent, intelligent, imaginative (and sometimes introverted) member, who often feels frustrated at the pace of group work. The ideas person is a source of new approaches to old problems, new ideas and strategies. The innovator likes puzzles, patterns, and problem-solving. The team values its innovator for independent outlook, as well as intelligence and imagination. An innovator's weaknesses are relatively tolerable: a tendency to be impractical, carelessness with details, or weakness at communicating ideas to members with different outlooks and attitudes.

e. *The Critic* (Belbin's 'Monitor–Evaluator'). This is the analyst, the careful, critical member, often slow but right. The critic's judgement wins over feelings, and his or her contributions are analysing problems and evaluating other people's ideas and suggestions. It is useful to have someone who can poke holes in unsound proposals before they have cost a lot. The critic is a necessary part of quality checking. The critic also wants to be sure all the information is at hand before a decision is made. This member is long on evaluation and objectivity, but probably too serious, unexciting, and occasionally *too* critical. It is best to send him or her away to do something useful elsewhere when the team is at the creative stage of problem-solving.

f. *The Implementer* (Belbin's 'Company Worker'). This is the practical type who turns ideas into manageable tasks, meeting targets and deadlines. The implementer wants clear objectives and procedures, and is sometimes uncomfortable with new ideas. This is the solid, systematic, trustworthy member who can make a practical plan to achieve the objective when the others have finished arguing about it. The team needs its implementer to turn concepts and plans into practical working procedures, and to carry them out methodically. Implementer strengths include self-control and self-discipline, realism, and common sense. This member may be a little inflexible or unexciting, perhaps unresponsive to new ideas that are not yet proven, but the implementer is probably the best at administration.

g. *The Team Builder* (Belbin's 'Team Worker'). This is the nurturer, the one who likes people and works easily with them, even when their ideas differ. The team builder will hold the team together, supporting the others in their strengths and filling in for their weaknesses, while oiling their communication machinery. The team builder is more concerned with the process than the precise result (where the shaper concentrates on the task itself, less concerned with the process). Strengths include listening, encouraging, harmonising. The team builder is characterised by flexibility, humility and popularity. These may be balanced by a lack of decisiveness or toughness, and a dislike for competition and friction among team members.

h. *The Finisher* This is one of the most important, and often least appreciated, members of the team. While the ideas man or the innovator starts things, the finisher completes them. This member's fine eye for detail is most likely to notice omissions or mistakes. The finisher checks details and schedules, makes sure the team makes few errors, and keeps track of the parts of the task that need extra attention. He or she also maintains a sense of urgency, and acts as the team's conscience. Failing enough current problems, the finisher will worry about future problems. Strengths include a sense of order, a well-focused purpose, self-control and strength of character. Foibles include impatience, intolerance to more casual members, and an inability to suffer fools or foolishness gladly.

Adjusting Team Balance

There are more elaborate (and expensive) ways to obtain accurate team role profiles: some have computerised scoring systems, while others have longer, more sophisticated 'instruments'. But there are also cheaper ways. Review the descriptions above and decide for yourself what you are – and guess about your fellow team members. Then check up and discuss your roles. This instrument may help the process by putting numbers on it, but most people know themselves well enough to choose the appropriate categories.

Sharing the team role information, and using it to sharpen the team's performance, is the real breakthrough.

Most people are able to fill more than one of these roles. In any group from five to ten or fifteen, the roles can be shared out if balance is maintained.

Problems can arise when a strong manager chooses too many members just like himself in his (or her) team. (Warren Bennis called this 'The *Doppelgänger* Effect' when he was writing about Richard Nixon's team – members of a team often model themselves on the leader, even to the brand of cigarettes they smoke.) A team of 'ideas men' doesn't want a finisher throwing cold water on their constructions. A practical team of implementers does not appreciate the butterfly 'contacts man'.

The first step to balancing a team is appreciating and respecting the natural styles of the other members. If everyone fills out the Inventory, and then they put their scores on to a single flip chart, the overlaps and gaps will show up immediately. You can fill gaps by finding the members whose second or third choices were highest in those categories, but there will have to be conscious discussion on ways to help them fill the underrepresented roles.

Except for the potential power problems between the chairman and shaper, there is no harm if more than one member prefers a particular role – perhaps taking turns to be the chief critic, or monitoring and evaluating different aspects of a project. As with marriage, it is the process of discussing and negotiating, bringing the differences to the surface, that makes them manageable. (Indeed, the team role approach can be useful in families, too.)

Whenever the project changes, or the team feels a bit frustrated, it's useful to haul out the team role flipchart and see whether all the roles are still being covered effectively. It can also be useful when a new member comes in, or when two teams share a project.

The Temporary Team

In addition to exploring the workings of *doppelgängers*, Warren Bennis wrote a significant book[4] on temporary structures: project teams, task forces, and other groups that would self-destruct when they had finished their work. In an increasingly bureaucratic world, we need to pay more attention to these ideas. Very few organisations today can afford the plethora of permanent structures that have grown up in response to temporary problems.

IBM has always been particularly effective at using temporary structures for a number of purposes:

- reinforcing the corporate culture;
- recognising achievement;
- solving problems;
- building networks.

IBM's 'task forces' are legendary. Like Japan's 'heavyweight' teams, these are led at a high level, have all the resources they need (and 'subpoena power' to tap the right people or information). Membership is viewed as an accolade, and the teams usually take the name of the leader or the project. Typically, a full-time task force might work for several months on a market or product problem, report its findings and recommendations to the board, and then dissolve itself, except for a few scheduled monitoring meetings.

A few project teams can be found in most organisations, but they are too often lightweight – part time, undersupported, not regarded highly enough by top management. They try strenuously to get a project off the ground, but time and weight of other tasks spells failure and guilt and lip-service. Like the 'customer charters' that abound today, these under-resourced projects are often an ambivalent top manager's protection from personal blame.

One large organisation put most of its management teams through an excellent sheep-dip quality training programme that included action planning for each team to start a project they were going to undertake jointly when they got back to work. Soon they had a huge population of managers who believed that their own lack of organisation and focus had made the projects fail. Then the chief executive decided to invest in his people by sending the rest of the workforce on a half-day version of the sheep-dip. The individual guilts were thus multiplied, but people were no more empowered or resourced to make needed changes.

Organisations need teams, not just to do the work but also to free them from the bureaucracy that people have created over the years. An individual may not have the confidence to tackle 'the system' when it is obstructive, but a well-motivated team can get round or over most hurdles. Teams, in turn, need turned on, well-trained members capable of further development, and one of the best forms of development I know is to take part in a worth-while team project.

The Japanese (and best Western companies) know that the best reward for solving a problem is being awarded another problem to solve. Organisational problems, however, tend to be too large and too complex for a single superman to tackle. Why not extend the concept of teams, and develop the members at the same time, by creating temporary but heavyweight teams to do the most crucial problem-solving?

Notes

1. Steven Wheelwright and Kim Clark (1992), *Revolutionizing Product Development*, New York: Free Press.

2. R. Meredith Belbin (1981), *Management Teams*, Oxford: Butterworth-Heinemann.

3. Nancy Foy (1980), *The Yin and Yang of Organizations*, London: Grant McIntyre; New York: Morrow

4. Warren Bennis (1968), *The Temporary Society*, New York: Harper & Row.

4

Visible Leadership

It takes a good leader to empower people. Without confidence in their leader, people feel that it is too dangerous to take responsibility on to their own shoulders. It is easy to ignore or shrug off empowering opportunities.

People want to be led. They want to be aware of leadership from the top; they want to see and hear the managers responsible for decisions that affect them; and they want day-by-day leadership from their own supervisors. If that leadership, at any level, assumes the parent role – 'father knows best' – then the only possible response for the employee is the child's – 'indeed, father knows best', whether it be an obedient or a naughty child's role.

Requirements for Leadership

Peter Drucker[1] says there are three requirements for leadership.

The leader's first task is to be the trumpet that sounds a clear sound.

What distinguishes the leader from the misleader are his goals. Whether the compromise he makes with the constraints of reality are compatible with his mission and goals or lead away from them determines whether he is an effective leader. And whether he holds fast to a few basic standards (exemplifying them in his own conduct) or whether 'standards' for him are what he can get away with, determines whether the leader has followers or only hypocritical time-servers.

Drucker's second requirement is that the leader sees his leadership as a responsibility, rather than rank and privilege. When things go wrong, the real leader does not blame others – 'the buck stops here'.

That kind of leader can empower people. He (or she) is not afraid of strength in subordinates; he wants and needs able, independent, self-assured people around him, and he sees their triumphs as his own, not as threats.

Drucker's third requirement of leadership is to earn trust. Discussions have to be consistent, or there will be no followers. Members of staff don't have to agree with the leader, or even like him, but they have to believe that he means what he says.

The American management guru Warren Bennis has done a considerable amount of work on developing the picture of the manager as coach – who must be, of course, empowered himself before he can empower his people. In a picture that echoes Drucker's 'requirements', Bennis describes leadership in terms of the leader's actions:

- motivating people to achieve;
- licensing them to tell the truth;
- fusing concept and detail.

Leaders *v.* Managers

The person who can become a leader and escape the traps of the culture or 'context' has the best chance of creating his own context; which is one of the important things leaders do for their people.

Are leaders made or born? There is certainly an element of luck, being in the right place at the right time, but never forget the old adage: 'Chance favours the prepared mind.' Bennis lists more characteristics needed by great leaders – the ones who take their chances and reach the top:

- Vision: the clear idea of what you want to do (and why) and the strength to persist until you get it.
- Passion: 'The leader loves what he does, and loves doing it.' The passion (or enthusiasm) he projects is what inspires others.
- Integrity: which combines self-knowledge, candour and maturity. 'You are your own raw material. When you know what you consist of and what you want to make of it, then you can invent yourself.' The leader with integrity can afford to develop it in others.
- Curiosity: the leader wonders about everything, wants to learn as much as he can, from every experience, good and bad.
- Daring: the leader takes risks, tries new things, doesn't worry too much about failure, learns from adversity.

To these five qualities I would add an important sixth:

- Generosity: the leader is confident enough and generous enough to empower and develop his or her subordinates. He or she really understands that great achievements demand the efforts of more than one person.

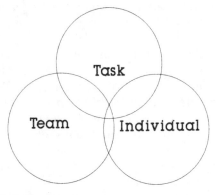

Figure 4.1 Action-centred Leadership

There are other lists of 'qualities of leadership', but very few experts disagree about what leaders do: their key tasks all demand communicating (especially listening), and delegating.

Author and consultant John Adair[2] studied what good leaders actually did, and developed a model which had three elements, described as

- building the team (nobody can gainsay that – it must happen);
- achieving the task (the reason the team exists); and
- developing the individuals (the investment that gives long-term returns).

It is the leader's job to control these often-diverging and always demanding phenomena. Adair developed a functional approach:

- define the task;
- plan;
- communicate;
- control;
- evaluate;
- motivate;
- organise;
- set an example.

The development task is just as crucial at the front line as it is for the top leader. At either level the leader should also be coach, facilitator, trainer, yet a survey in one large company showed only 15 per cent of employees saw their front-line manager as trainer or coach.

A number of experts distinguish between 'leaders' and 'managers', and it is tempting to do so. People want to be 'led', but few people would say they want to be 'managed'. Bennis sees the leader as 'whole brain,' using imagination, open, taking risks, versus the manager as 'left brain', closed, using common-sense, obeying rules. Those are different groups of people, in his scheme.

Another split might be like 'ladies' and 'women' – all leaders are managers, but not all managers are leaders.

I still have reservations, for I believe that any manager needs at least a few qualities of leadership, the ability to get people to do things. Front-line managers and top managers probably need extra-strong leadership qualities, because they must constantly convey to their people that vision and passion. Adair's model, with its eye on the task, makes it clear what you have to do about it, for he is talking about activities and you can teach activity. You are out of the 'born leader' concept, and into the world where leaders can be made. (Adair notes that many people can take decisions – that is straightforward in most cases – but the leader's individual style is a more important part of the recipe.)

The current approaches to developing leadership neglect at least 80 per cent of potentially good leaders, who accidentally (or by choice) do not acquire opportunities. The number of able people stuck (by accident or choice) at the supervisor level suggests that front-line managers may show more deference than the top managers – many seem willing to forgo extra inward–upward competition in favour of the rewards of having a stable 'patch of turf' of one's own to tend. The good leader is not necessarily the ambitious 'A-type', overflowing with drive and enthusiasm. A lazy, easygoing 'B-type' problem-avoider can usually achieve a task as effectively and often with less hassle and expense than his 'A-type counterpart.*

A real leader can say to his people, 'I don't know, but I'll find out and come back to you.'

To me, that is the mark of openness, confidence, credibility – the first step towards trust – and those are the qualities the empowerer needs.

The Coherent Organisation

The organisation that can empower its leaders in these directions, and support them with a performance focus and two-way planning, will gain not only in concepts like 'motivation', but in the hard, clear, business-led achievement that motivation and leadership can bring.

In an empowering organisation there is coherence and consist-

*Research shows that 'A-types' suffer more from heart-attacks than anything else.

ency between what people learn on the ground, and what the top leaders say, whether it be face to face, on video, in the house journal, or on the local radio station. The trouble is, there are too few large empowering organisations. Ambivalence is normal, for organisations as well as individuals, when it comes to shifting real power out towards the front line.

Signals from the Top

The signals employees listen to from the top leadership are the same as the ones they listen to from other levels:

- Who gets hired?
- Who gets fired?
- Why?
- Where are we really going?

Board members are managers: they just have more management responsibility than anybody else. The board is totally responsible for the organisation. Even for a government body , or a hospital unit, the top group has to take decisions and point the directions, with enough vision and passion to get through the 'felted' layers of managers in the middle who have learned to resist change.

The managers at the top do not always realise the gimlet-eyed attention people further down the organisation pay to appointments. Bringing in a new executive can symbolize a great deal of change. They ought to make sure that all the managers down the line can go out and tell their people first hand what the board wants, and why.

Top Leadership Tasks

It is the job of top management to make conditions right to empower the front line, and ultimately the organisation.

A few leaders at the top may recognise the near-impenetrable layers between themselves and the employees they need to empower. What, then can be done? Reorganise them out? Fire the culprits? Or find the exceptions?

In my experience, the few great change programmes that worked in large organisations have come about from short circuits, initiatives that connected the top to the bottom, sparked by leaders like Tom Watson at IBM (and a generation later Tom Jr), Johan Holte at Norsk Hydro, or Pehr Gyllenhammar at Volvo. The exceptional leaders who can create and maintain empowering short cuts through the felted layers of communication filters between themselves and their people at the front line fit the Drucker and Bennis leadership models. Those I have known have also been willing to cause discomfort to their subordinates at many levels when they can see scope for improvements for the organisation as a whole.

People in organisations need to go around channels as well as through them. In most organisations attempts to create short cuts skip the front-line manager. The most important source of empowering is eroded, diminished, made less credible.

Notes

1. Peter Drucker, 'Leadership: More Doing Than Dash', *Wall Street Journal*, 6 January 1988.

2. John Adair (1983), *Effective Leadership*, Aldershot: Gower.

5

Good Communication

You can't empower people until they know what's going on in the organisation.

You can't achieve real quality until everyone feels informed. You can't change a culture or make an organisation more flexible until you get two-way, face-to-face internal communication right.

Communication is the bedrock underpinning any organisational change.

The Primary Building Block

Picture an organisation where people believe most of what the company tells them. The company, in turn, listens to what the employees are concerned about, and tries to answer their questions. Work groups meet regularly to discuss what is going on and review their performance. In this ideal organisation the grapevine and trade union information are roughly the same as the information that reaches people through their own supervisors – who usually hear and tell it first. The top managers walk about regularly, and know not only the names of most employees, but how their teams are performing. The employees, in turn, feel that their efforts to improve performance are recognized and appreciated.

Why should this picture be an ideal, rather than a reality?

Good communication does not mean that *all* information is in the public domain. People need to know enough to run the organisation, and enough is different for different people. We feed from the same information trough, but we take in different amounts, and process it differently, each through our own experience. One person's 'truth' is another's 'propaganda', depending on one's experience filter. So you have to have enough information 'food' in the trough to cover everyone's different appetite. Some people pay no attention to something until they have heard it three or four times, from different sources; others try to file everything. Thus you need a broad base of available information. Colin Minton expresses it as an equation:

$$Openness = broad\ base + multiple\ access$$

Even if your base is broad, and everyone has access, you still have to worry about the flavour.

Me, Us and Them

In communication there seems to be a hierarchy of needs. People want most of all to know what concerns them personally: the 'me' information. Only after that need is filled do they have energy and interest to listen to things about 'us', 'our group', 'our achievements'. And only when 'me' and 'us' are taken care of can you expect them to give any attention to 'them' information.

In a typical organisation, on the other hand, the people originating formal communications are usually headquarters managers, whose 'me' information tends to be financial control, or corporate profit or politics. In the eyes of employees out at the sharp end, that is all 'Monopoly money', markers in someone else's game.

The 'me' information at the sharp end is reassurance that people are not going to be laid off – something headquarters seldom remembers to reassure people about, especially in Britain in the 1990s.

I actually believe the current recession would end in a flash if the leaders of the country's largest organisations locked themselves away together to bite all the bullets at once, then came home and insisted that their managers put all their plans and worries on paper. At the end of a month, every employee would receive a letter saying:

> The earliest we can conceive your personal sell-by date will be October 1995, and we expect your unit to go on operating until at least April 1997. If you have plans for personal development, it may help you to know that we expect to slim down the whole organisation by 13 per cent per year for the foreseeable future. Therefore, if you are interested in taking early retirement, we expect the following terms to be available:

followed by a table of ages, years of service, pension entitlement, and early retirement terms. This would give people the basis for making 'me' decisions, as well as the good and bad information they need to stop spending so much time reading imaginary tea-leaves for clues to the 'me' and 'us' future. Most of them would sigh with relief and immediately go out and buy the washing machine or microwave oven they've been deferring.

As it stands now, when an organisation is known to be reducing its workforce by 10 per cent over the next five years, 80 per cent of its people think this means that their own jobs will disappear next year – so no one is buying cars, or television sets, or houses.

Job security is the most elemental 'me'. Once that worry is out of the way, all employees want answers to just four simple questions:

1. *How am I doing?*
   How are we doing?
   How is the organisation doing?

2. *What standards do they expect of me?*
   To what standards are we working?
   To what standards is the organisation working?

3. *Where am I going?*
    Where are we going?
    Where is the organisation going?

4. *How will I get there?*
    How will we get there?
    How will the organisation get there?

Communication	Me	Us	Them
Progress			
Standards			
Direction			
Means			

Figure 5.1 Communication Matrix

To respond to this matrix, you need measures, at each level. One company has elegant measures of performance, based on what their customers say, yet they keep it secret for fear the shareholders, the unions, and other stakeholders will hold it against them when performance is less than perfect. Another company fears the City analysts, who hold no stake at all.

Organisations compete for their employees' attention with every form of external media – television, radio, newspapers, special interests, and so on. People have only limited time and patience and attention to spare, so they will spend it in the ways most fruitful and interesting to them. If what the organisation releases about their work is slick, boring, or old, they will lose interest. Most would rather know more about their favourite soap opera on television than about the people in the next department. No matter how much a company exports, the staff view of international business will be based on *Dallas*, not the company's results.

In Glasgow's Albany Hotel, someone once asked a bellhop: 'Is the hotel full?' He responded: 'Eighty-three point five per cent occupancy, sir!' The surprised guest mentioned the well-informed employee to the manager, who said that a few months before, he had found out that his staff knew more about a mythical motel on television called 'Crossroads' than they knew about the Albany. So he began to brief them every morning about the state of the Albany business.

Keeping everyone informed can be an elaborate and expensive business. When John Egan was leader at Jaguar in the 1980s he introduced a comprehensive structure of communications:

- weekly executive meetings;
- monthly management committee review of communications;
- company objectives cascaded, as a basis for appraisal;
- bimonthly management conferences, all levels (with minutes circulated as a basis for briefing staff);
- weekly briefing groups (fed by the plant directors' weekly meetings with all their supervisors);
- quality circles, backed by monthly suggestion awards;
- formal employee relations including information meetings and joint consultation meetings with unions – many initiated by management;
- full-time management of the above, plus video, company newsletter, monthly management bulletin, noticeboards, plant briefs, poster campaigns, management newsclippings, and the like;
- a 'hearts and minds' programme including sports, social activities, open days, previews of new models, preretirement services, open learning with formal qualifications, and so on.

This did not stop Jaguar sales going into a terrible slump when currency changes affected exports but it certainly helped achieve the revival of the firm when the currency crisis eased.

Peter Drucker wrote in 1987[1]

> In today's corporations – or, for that matter, hospitals, universities and other institutions – there are far too many layers of management. Most importantly, this affects communications. There is a communications theorem that every relay doubles the noise and cuts the message in half. This applies to humans as much as to cables. Moreover, additional relays delay communications.

The Credible Manager

The credibility of the organisation and its top management rests entirely in the hands of the lowly front-line manager. When people believe that their own supervisors know what is going on, they usually believe that most managers up the line also know what they are doing, and that the company is being open with them.

One 'secret' of Japanese management, available to anyone else who notices it, is the attention they pay to maintaining management credibility. The Japanese understand the gap between *de facto* and *de jure* what is, and what is 'legislation' or claimed. Japanese companies seldom count on the big announcement or publication of a new organisation chart to trigger new relationships. Instead, they introduce changes, little by little, until they have grown the new organisation they want. Only after everyone knows all the words and all the tunes to the new company anthems do the leaders stand up in public to direct the chorus.

Too often in the Western world, headquarters tells the whole world it is going to do something – before they bother to tell their own managers. The formal communications machinery in a large organisation can set off concerns and discomforts throughout the organisation, long before elaborate claims for change have a chance to come true. Reorganisations become counter-productive when they create a year or two of massive insecurity.

If you want change, you often have to claim slightly more than you have previously delivered. You have to stretch a little, to set targets that are ambitious, but not impossible. This applies to groups and organisations as well as individuals. To learn, they have to try something new. But we live in an increasingly insecure world, where people want everything safe.

People are sometimes fired for telling the truth: 'murdering the messenger who brings bad tidings'. The leaders who have thus deprived themselves of bad news (or reality) can be dangerous. They tell subordinates to set tough targets – then add another 10 per cent just to keep people 'on their toes'. This can catapult an organisation into the credibility chasm.

A manager's credibility does not necessarily drop gradually: a single event can send it plunging over a cliff. The leader who did not want to listen to bad news, or his subordinate who was not allowed to tell it, made one promise too many, imposed a 'tough target' that was demotivating because it was unattainable.

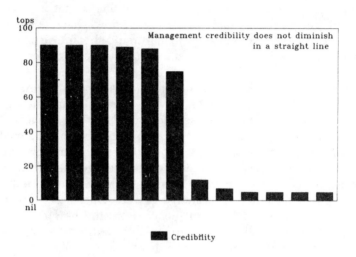

Figure 5.2 Management Credibility

Nissan's Road to Credibility

Nissan started in the UK with a greenfield site near Newcastle during the 1980s. After careful screening for attitudes as well as experience, excellent foremen were chosen and trained. They, in turn, helped select the members of their work teams. The entire focus of the company is on teamwork and commitment.

Striving for 'commitment' rather than 'control', Nissan managers developed a philosophy statement which was signed by its managing director, and issued to every employee. Personnel Director Peter Wickens calls it 'the point to which we aim to return when blown off course'. The statement says:

> 'We will develop and expand the contribution of all staff by strongly emphasising training and the expansion of everyone's capabilities.

We seek to delegate and involve staff in discussion and decision-making, particularly in those areas in which they can effectively contribute so that all may participate in the efficient running of [the company].

Within the bounds of commercial confidentiality we would like everyone to know what is happening in our company, how we are performing and what we plan.

We want information and views to flow freely upward, downward and across our company.'

Nissan views a five-minute meeting every morning as the most important aspect in building both teamwork and commitment. This is how Peter Wickens[2] describes it:

'Every day the foreman talks *with* his people. This talk is frequently about quality but it will also be used to discuss schedule changes, work redistribution, process changes, training, the introduction of a new member or social events. Sometimes, team members other than the foreman will cover certain points. Most of the discussion is about matters that directly affect the team in their daily work and will originate from the supervisor himself. . . . The philosophy is that if something is worth telling it should be told immediately and the best method of communication is face to face. . . . Not only does this give immediacy but also develops [the supervisor's] role as the genuine leader of the group. He who communicates is king!'

The Nissan meetings take place in each team's meeting area, where the supervisor has his desk, with lockers, tables, benches, blackboards, notice-boards, recreational facilities, and tea- or coffee-making facilities. Tea breaks are team-building, too. Several times a day, one member normally stops early to make the tea, and they get block relief for the rest of the team to gather together, often replanning processes and reviewing progress informally as they sip. Wickens wrote, 'Essential to this process is an acceptance on the part of managers and supervisors that they have no monopoly of wisdom on the best way of performing a task or on making improvements.'

If something happens that members of a Nissan team ought to know, the supervisor goes around telling them: 'We'll have a chance to discuss it more in the morning.'

A Communication Strategy

The organisations which manage communication decently tend to have thought the concept through far more than just who is to edit the house journal. There are key strategic questions that need to be addressed:

- Who owns communication? The answers here must take into account the commitment of top management, the trade union role, and the history and culture of the organisation. Without a very clear answer, communication will bog down in politics.
- How are managers to be accountable? This is a question that tends to evolve as communications develop, but it ought to be addressed at the outset – as the BT case in Chapter 19 demonstrates, a focus on employee communication actually changes the definition of good management.
- Communication management costs money. Is the organisation willing to pay for the full-time manager it usually takes? The absence of such management, however, is even more expensive!
- What upward and downward channels will be used? The mix should fit into existing channels and make them more credible.
- Concentrate on face-to-face communication. Like Nissan, I am convinced that this is the key to any effective communication strategy. The credibility of the top manager rests on the effectiveness of the front-line manager.
- Communicate the entitlement. People *are* entitled to know what is expected of them and how they are doing. Is the organisation willing to publish its communication policy, with the success that it expects? If so, it has to implement enough improvements for the policy itself to be credible.

The Communication Manager

The 'sheep-dog' communication manager herds his charges safely into the fold. The 'bird-dog' seeks out the target (in this case excellence, not dead birds) and perseveres until higher authority pays attention. The 'walking cane' supports management walkabout until it becomes a natural daily activity. This guardian of management credibility is an absolute necessity if an organisation wants to improve employee communications. An 'unmanaged' process will naturally wilt when it meets competition for resources, attention and time from more proactively sponsored programs.

In any organisation with more than a few hundred people, I do not think the communication manager can do the job on a part-time basis, for it is one of the most important tasks in improving an organisation. Communication is essential for quality, customer care, profit, efficiency, effectiveness – all the things top teams say they want.

Communication managers tend to become change agents as they gain a wider view of the issues that concern people from top to bottom. They can come from a variety of backgrounds, but in my view the best ones are closest to their clients: the supervisors in the mainstream of the business.

In many companies there is a tendency to put employee communication somewhere between Personnel (which owns the 'messages') and Marketing or PR (which usually owns the 'machinery' for communicating with employees). Either way, you have a problem.

- Personnel has a natural aversion to telling people things – 'Don't make waves!'
- Marketing and PR want to 'prettify' what they have to say. They will put a good editor in the job.

Communication means warts-and-all, telling the truth. This is the only way to create the open, trusting atmosphere in which teams and commitment can grow. Managing communication is not an editorial task; it requires the ability to face up to senior executives, sometimes with uncomfortable information. Here are some of the tasks I would expect this paragon to carry out:

- organise face-to-face meeting systems;
- make sure that managers manage their own communication;
- follow up, follow through;

- eradicate red tape;
- serve as a 'walking cane' (or scribe) and 'bird dog', sniffing out excellence for senior management recognition
- serve as a 'sheep dog', training and coaching managers in communication skills, nudging them in the right direction;
- monitor and measure results.

If you are not going to have a proper full-time communication manager, then at least assign the part-time task to a highly motivated person in a core location – the MD's secretary, perhaps, or a key receptionist.

No matter from what level the communication manager comes, a crucial aspect of the job, at least in the first few months, will be regular and serious access to the top executive. It can be helpful, too, if the top team reviews communication on its normal agendas.

Notes

1. Peter Drucker (1987), 'Personal View', *Strategic Planning Society News*, July/Aug. 1987.

2. Peter Wickens (1987), *The Road to Nissan*, Basingstoke: Macmillan.

Part II

How to Manage Empowerment

Every meaningful model for change includes the basic elements of empowerment:

- performance;
- teams;
- leadership;
- communication.

You'd think we'd have learned by now! Yet look how organisations large and small have mismanaged change:

- Only 20 per cent of 'Total Quality Management' programmes succeed.
- 'Team briefing' usually silts up with top-down bumf.
- 'Employee involvement' is mainly sheep-dip training and consultancy fees.
- 'Customer Care'? Often no more than plastic smiles and platitudes.

What makes the difference? The commitment of top management

needs to be demonstrated more vividly, not on the video, but in actions that speak louder than words.

What follows is the nuts-and-bolts, how-to-do-it section of the book. It examines the steps to empowerment, and some of the obstacles.

6

Plans and Strategies

Higher does not necessarily mean wiser. What might help is subsidiarity – doing things and taking decisions at the lowest possible level. If it were wholeheartedly carried out in normal organisations subsidiarity would give them better performance. There are ways to make it happen more often.

Change, at any level, needs a blueprint – a picture of where we are, where we want to go, and how we are going to get there. Developing that picture can be a useful process, involving everyone who has information or concerns to share. There are ways to make it happen more often.

Small is Beautiful

In *Small is Beautiful*[1] E. F. Schumacher noted a difference between plans and predictions:

> To apply the word 'planning' to matters outside the planner's control is absurd. Events, as far as the planner is concerned, simply happen. He may be able to forecast them and this may well influence his plan; but they cannot possibly be part of the plan.

A plan is a statement of intention, of what the planners (or their masters – or their minions) intend to do. Schumacher said that planning is inseparable from power.

The further ahead the planner looks, and the wider the territory his plan covers, the more his power. Yet the further ahead a forecast reaches, the more likely it is to be blown off course by unplanned events.

Planners are seldom held to account for their previous forecasts – doers usually get blamed instead. Yet what is to stop any organisation creating a league table of planners, according to their 'plan/actual ratio' for the past two or five or ten years?

In a twisted manifestation of 'small is beautiful', IBM, with some of the best long-range planning in the world, could not forecast its loss of market control through the awesome leap of the personal computer from company tool to consumer product (the busiest corner in most newsagents these days is usually the computer magazine shelf.) Many product planners will testify that runaway successes have been 'happy accidents'.

It is much easier to plan whether my family will have a new PC this year or next. My small-scale, short-term forecast is sturdier than their large-scale, long-term forecast.

Power to the Planners

Most large organisations are notable for a 'great divide', by which members of the culture recognise each other. IBM split historically into Domestic and World Trade. Philips was Commercial or Technical. Unilever people were Food or Soap. More than one giant organisation I know has its cultural wall right down the middle of every single activity: a separation between planning and doing.

At some time in the past [in that 'We know what's best for you' tone of organisation voice that reminds me of prissy British headmasters] large organisations decided that the people out in the field would not be working at full capacity unless there were experts in the centre to plan their work and tell them how long it would take. This is a natural extension of the success Henry Ford and others had with Frederick Taylor's stopwatches and clipboards.

Once the planners are in place, creative people that they are, they begin to invent more and more elaborate systems to control the doers. Doers, in turn, invent more and more elaborate ways (or 'events') to subvert the plans. Information chasms grow up between the planners and doers. [Mao must have recognised this when he sent the bureaucrats out into the fields during the Cultural Revolution.]

When somebody else does your planning for you, it deprives you of responsibility for the plan, and of the satisfaction of meeting targets you have helped set for yourself. Your 'power' suffers as that of the planners increases.

Most planning is seen from below as a top-down imposition. In an empowering organisation, however, planning could be part of every worker's job description. Leaders higher up simply have to plan a little further ahead, because they have more workers to co-ordinate and support.

This is a gentle approach to defining 'strategy'. In truth, I think the lines between plans and tactics and strategies are artificial and divisive, not helpful to the organisation at all.

A few organisations, like Xerox, have managed to make planning a live process, rolling performance information and resource plans up, then using the larger-scale and longer-term picture to negotiate nearer-term and more local plans, within agreed frameworks. It can be a painful ritual imposed by the culture – but when every front-line manager or team leader has been involved in rolling the 6-month plan, or the 18-month plan, or the 5-year framework, each knows where his own team is going, and how its work fits into the plan.

Some organisations believe their strategies should be secret. Absurd! If nobody knows where the organisation's leaders want it to go, how can employees help them get there?

Defining the Problems

Most organisations behave as though 'strategy' belongs to the board (or its intimate associates) and mere 'tactics' belong to everyone else. Toyota turned this on its head at NUMMI and

convinced the jaded workforce that *they* were the strategic
resource – the difference between success and failure. It was
deeds, not words, that gained people's trust and involvement.
The workers were trained. Leaders were even more trained.
Teams were small, workable, and had the Taylor tools to improve
their own performance. Performance figures were posted for all
to see and better.

I like the Japanese management approach that spends a lot of
time involving everyone in definitions of the problem. Papers roll
up and down the organisation, gathering comments and
changes. This slow definition phase results in rapid implementation once everyone shares the well-developed, unified picture of
the problem.

BT has used outsiders as catalysts for internal co-ordination.
Inputs from customers and outside experts as well as inside
departments are used to tackle strategic problems in a way that
reminds me of the Japanese.

BT's problem-defining model came not from the Japanese, but
from Jan Walsh, manager of the company's Consumer Relations
Unit, which hosts a number of Consumer Liaison Panels. For a
topic like how to deal with malicious callers, for example, BT's
'Issues Exchange' started in 1990 with a one-day brainstorming
session that involved about a hundred internal and external
stakeholders working together in syndicates. Various participants explained the problem as they saw it; no decisions were
expected, just widely shared information and ideas.

The slow defining stage went on for a few one-day seminars,
each resulting in papers that defined or clarified more of the
problem, as well as related issues. If BT tackled malicious calls
with phones that can register the caller's phone number, how
would they be allocated and monitored? Privacy issues lurked,
and legal questions. After more than a year, a distillation of the
insiders and outsiders met with Mike Bett, the deputy chairman,
to propose the well-considered responses to the issue. He was
able to give an immediate go-ahead for a number of positive
steps, which happened in quick succession:

- BT helped increase public awareness of what to do if you
  receive a malicious call.
- It created a network of Malicious Call Bureaux, to counsel

customers who had been troubled and work with police to catch and prosecute offenders and generally coordinate the effort and personnel needed to solve these complex complaints.

- Caller Display (where your phone displays the telephone number of the person calling you), already under trial, might be another weapon in the fight to deter anonymous or malicious callers.

My Target, Our Plan, Their Strategy

From the board's viewpoint, strategy often involves moving work, winding up one group, starting another. Parts of the work are overtaken by technology – that is the most frequent and most valid reason.

The reason behind the reason often includes a desire not to attract trouble, not to create problems: peace at any price. The press, the City, the politicians – they all fuss so. As to the employees, no one wants to give people bad news, so the strategists wait somewhat longer than they should to let the cat out of the bag.

Look at British Coal these days. They used to be the forward-thinking National Coal Board which attracted the best organisational minds to help them make room for freedom and order in the same large organisation. Imagine an organisation that used and influenced Frits Schumacher, Jacob Bronowski, Reg Revans and a number of other innovators, looking for the magic combination of order and freedom to develop new enterprises and networks for entrepreneurship. What forces disabled the coal company's antennae to such an extent that closure announcements were made with absolutely no consultation with employees?

Very few 'events' are totally unpredictable. Big 'strategic' decisions often have to be made because small, incremental changes were not encouraged. Many of those smaller changes are often foreseen and even unsuccessfully proposed by people at lower- and middle-management levels.

People at the coalface do not want to take responsibility for strategic decisions to close a pit, or 30 pits. But they do want to be involved in setting their own practical targets, and seeing some benefit in meeting them. It should be management's job to make good connections between the two.

Incremental change, gradual change, is the bridge between their strategy, our plan, and my target.

If I help to set my target, and we take our targets together into our plan, then we have a good chance to achieve the short-term plan, and the organisation can depend on us. If they want to move a group, or try something new, a few of us could learn to do things differently, or work in a different place, adjusting our plans and targets.

Some Strategic Outputs

There are specific things top managers can do to show commitment to empowering, and to give people more room to make their own incremental changes. Using his ICI experience, Derek Sheane[2] suggests that the top of the organisation could try experiments like:

- Generate less unnecessary work by asking for less or different information.
- Do less, think more.
- Intervene less and counter their need to be busy.
- Help us by clarifying our purposes and priorities.

Valerie Stewart[3] asks the most strategic question of all: 'Have you really empowered your managers?' In *The David Solution* she offers a ten-point checklist for head office's part in empowering:

1. Are you responding more quickly to ideas and suggestions?
2. Are you really rewarding good ideas?
3. Have you delegated authority, or just delegated work?
4. Have managers the freedom not to rely on head office at all?
5. Are you seeking uniformity and conformity for its own sake?
6. Do you issue rules, or do you discuss principles?
7. Systems can be a frame or a cage.
8. If the system is to be broken, where is the burden of proof?
9. Diluting local priorities means diluting local authority.
10. Is the customer's voice heard?

Strategy for Empowering

When you are planning empowerment, communications, quality
– things that depend on credible management and everyone's
belief – everyone needs to see how the plan is developed.
Everyone needs to understand what it is for, and why the
organisation wants it. Gently, without too much publicity,
everyone needs to be enticed into taking part in the process.

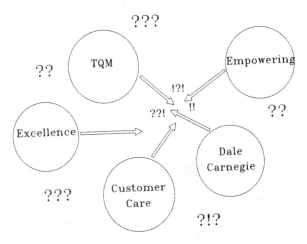

Figure 6.1 Conflicting Change Programmes

Remember how the 'role' model encourages uproar, while the
'task' model helps get things done. It may help a co-ordinating
group (a better name than 'planning' or 'strategy team') to review
the present situation for themselves to work with top management to develop a 'leading edge' for change. Communication,
and quality, and empowerment, and customer focus, and
performance, and excellence share many of the same elements,
but claims for them can get in each other's way. They often have
different owners in the organisation, so petty politics intrudes.

With a single 'leading edge', energy is concentrated and the
many related goals (not 'programmess'!) have a better chance of
being achieved.

'Everyone' is not going to develop the strategy. That needs to

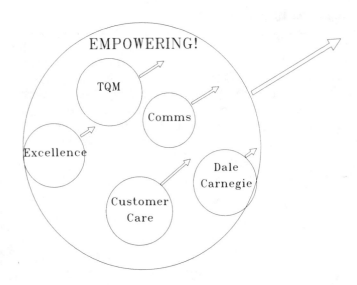

Figure 6.2 Leading Edge for Change

be in the hands of a credible few. They need to look at the strategic questions:

1. Where is empowering (communication . . .) now?
2. How much empowering (communication . . .) do we want?
3. How are we going to achieve it?

That first question is the key to wider involvement. If, at this stage, everyone has a chance to contribute, through group meetings or a survey with feedback and discussion, then a Japanese-style process can begin as people share their definitions of the problem.

Empowerment strategy is particularly susceptible; it will not work if it is developed in a vacuum. On the other hand, neither will it work if it is a glossy pamphlet with full-colour photos of the board; 'Empower!' it proclaims, and top executives wait for things to start happening. The pamphlet falls into the abyss of hypocrisy because it claimed too much too soon.

Notes

1. E. F. Schumacher (1973), *Small is Beautiful*, London: Blond & Briggs.

2. Derek Sheane (1976), *Beyond Bureaucracy*, Bolton, Lancs: Management Research.

3. Valerie Stewart (1990), *The David Solution*, Aldershot: Gower.

7

Whose Culture?

People need a sense of membership, of belonging to each other and to something larger than themselves. 'Culture' is the collection of symbols and concepts they draw around themselves, in groups or organisations (or tribes, or nations) to reinforce that sense of membership.

What is Culture?

Culture often manifests itself in costume and artefacts – not just 'image clothing' or uniforms, but 'grey flannel suits', or bowlers and brollies, or twinsets and pearls, or cloth caps and bacon butties. In one office everyone has colourful posters on the walls, in another clean desks and orderly framed seascapes on bland beige walls are the norm. Down the road they run to pneumatic secretaries, dramatic potted philodendrons, mahogany panelling and modern sculpture.

If we are 'in', then it helps define us more clearly if they are 'out' – just as finding a common enemy is a short cut to making friends (much faster than exploring the nuances of common friends). Within 30 seconds of the mutual recognition of a common enemy, you will have shared your values, risked something, and demonstrated that you trust the other person.

So culture is built on shared definitions of 'good' and 'bad', nowadays vaunted as 'values'. The ultimate punishment in every culture I know is to be cast out of the culture – excommunication, banishment, being fired.

In many cautious cultures, the individual who rejects the culture, who leaves of his own accord, is viewed as dangerous, and *post facto* regarded as 'bad'. Thus many organisations deprive themselves of outside experience by forbidding re-entry to adventurous ex-members.

The 'Culture Change' Conundrum

'Culture change' programmes are on sale like soap powder. Phalanxes of consultants make fortunes with culture change packages (usually starting with a five-figure diagnostic phase, which is the consultant's licence to find out what your people have been trying to tell you for ages).

Nonsense! *The culture belongs to its members, not to its managers.* Like Topsy, it just grows. It changes only slowly, because culture is the accumulated belief of all the members about who they are and what they stand for. Like 'image', culture has as many facets as there are people who perceive it, experience it, or make it. Even if you change a massive proportion of the systems and management styles, the perceptions of the people will persist for several years.

In most organisations people's beliefs about crime, punishment, sin and redemption can stop things changing, no matter how much management tells them that transformation is under way.

How can organisations seriously contemplate 'culture change' programmes, when a Unilever manager, after 35 years in ice cream, can still tell you he's really a 'soap man' at heart?

The Real Elements of Culture

A nation's culture, or that of a family, or an organisation, is made up of the stories that tell us who we are and where we came from, how people like us behave under various circumstances. I dislike the overworked word 'values' because it has come to mean a top-down value statement that seldom changes any behaviour, whereas the values of a culture underpin people's perceptions.

I remember wondering why people in Shell seldom used the word 'manager'. One had 'administrator' on his passport. Another's was 'oil company executive', and a third called himself 'chemical engineer' after 25 years in the higher echelons of general management. I finally met a finance man of advanced years who knew the roots. 'I think it was during the 1950s,' he recalled. He thought the government of the time imposed, for only a few months, a ruling that a company which 'managed' foreign subsidiaries had to take their profits into its accounts. Shell (very responsive to governments) rapidly discovered it had no managers, only administrators or co-ordinators. The value on the new words remained long after the formal cause, the government ruling, had disappeared. The roots, relatively trivial or ephemeral, are long since forgotten, but the company's language changed permanently.

Culture is a mix of myths, moral tales, larger-than-life characters, heroes, villains, martyrs, sin and redemption fables, and the odd bit of witchcraft – almost all of them elements outside the reach of management.

Heroes If you visit a Chinese factory you usually find a glass-fronted box outside by the gate, with large photographs of the current heroes, mounted for everyone to see. Groups can be heroes too, as the Japanese demonstrate with their quality programmes.

IBM, which has a particularly coherent corporate culture, used to have a very effective way of identifying heroes at every level. Every front-line manager had a small 'Recognition' budget (it used to be about £25 per person per year) to spend as he or she pleased on the 8–10 members of the group. Thus, the wives of three people who worked through two nights to finish a key report received flowers from the leader: 'Our culture values working through the night, as well as happy wives.' The person who had just completed a difficult sale was surprised with a gold pen presentation the next day: 'Selling is a Good Thing.'

A group of managers in another company brainstormed ways to recognise excellence (in other words, to tell their people who the organisation cherished, and why). Some of their ideas included:

- Use the house journal – printing photographs, not of the top managers, but of members of the workforce, with their full names.
- Loosen up the annual one-day management forum.
- Start an employee-of-the-month programme, with nominations from happy customers.
- Give heroic employees special uniforms.

The possibilities are endless, but seldom used.

Martyrs The person who is a hero in the eyes of his workmates (often for asking difficult questions which they value) can become enshrined in the corporate culture by being fired unfairly.

The higher up the organisation chart martyrdom occurs, the more profound the effect. Seldom do board members recognise the effect of high-level departures on corporate cultures, the strength of the signals these send out into the organisation. It can take years or even decades to repair morale after the departure of a well-regarded top manager.

Villains The person who is not a hero, and is fired fairly, can reinforce the message of 'who we aren't'. But more often the villains in a culture survive, such as the bully who ensures that he or she is the only one who knows how to run the accounting programs on the old mainframe. If we did not already have so many potential villains we might have to invent them, to unite the rest of the people and give them something to distract them from the dreariness of repetitive work.

Human Sacrifices When something goes wrong, the culture needs an explanation. It is tempting to pin the blame, personify it, then symbolically eliminate the 'bad', casting out the one who symbolises failure. The message is supposed to be: 'Now we have finished with poor-quality widgets. Let's get on with making Excellent widgets.'

The sacrifice often generates a different message, however. 'Henry tried to make widgets more efficiently, but he couldn't get the bugs out of the system fast enough. Therefore, let's not try anything new – we might get the blame if it doesn't work.' The number of CYA memos (memos from people who are trying to cover themselves) increases perceptibly. Meetings solve less and blame more. The culture has taken in the new message, and people behave accordingly.

Crime and Punishment What are the crimes for which our culture imposes the ultimate penalty? 'He wore *white socks*, too!' The word gets around. He wasn't 'us', so it's OK he's gone. He told lies – or he wouldn't tell the lies all the rest of us needed.

It is very useful to be able to punish people who break the cultural rules – and still retain their energy and loyalty. Very few organisations have mastered the trick. One of IBM's less-recognised strengths is deeply embedded in the culture: the offer of redemption to sinners.

When Gil Jones was number two in IBM, he used to go out and lecture about his time in the 'penalty box', IBM's widely recognised redemption mechanism, formally known as the International Sales Centre in New York City. Jones had committed the crime of cutting the number of customer service people in his region and generating too many customer complaints. He was sent to the penalty box, where he had little to do, no phone calls, no copies of papers or memos. For more than a year he was a non-person. Then a memo went out: Jones was assigned back to the real world, not promoted, but not demoted either. A few months later, he was back in the main line, just as full of zest, but a little wiser – and so were all his colleagues.

Myths Myths reinforce behaviour. In one sales-oriented company salespeople are quite certain they can be fired for 'over-selling' (pushing so hard it becomes visibly immoral), and for under-selling (not pushing hard enough to make their quota). The members understand the rather narrow plateau on which they operate, and do not seem to have much trouble with it.

Myths also grow up around promotions: 'You have to have marketing experience to get ahead around here.'

It has been said that the two purposes of religion are to explain the inexplicable, and to build patterns for social behaviour which enable people to survive in (relative) harmony.

The same is true, on a smaller scale, of organisational cultures. Members of a culture have to invent myths to explain things they do not understand: 'We know Gerry is useless, but he's just been promoted. You have to toady to get ahead here.'

A leading car company learned somewhat late about myth-making. The company had a Darwinian approach to development: survival of the fittest, in an environment where there were plenty of 'holes', gaps that gave opportunities for self-development. The trouble was that, when outside events like the oil crisis began to affect the industry, the holes gradually disappeared. Without anyone responsible for looking after the 'human resource', management noticed almost too late that even the best people had stopped moving upwards. People at the top never heard the new myths developing:

- If you aren't Grade 9 by the time you're 29, you'll never make it.
- I haven't been promoted; I don't have a degree.
- I don't have the right kind of degree.
- I'm too old.

Hundreds of able people who had been conditioned to peak performance at the prospect of 'getting ahead' began to sag. The zest oozed out of the organisation. More gloomy myths festered. The company's troubles today hark back to those myths.

Puberty Rites One of the myths people generated was: 'You can't get to the top without a stint in the field.' Field service in their company was a 16-hour-a-day slog, where staff were overworked, underpaid, and often divorced together. The young people who strove to obtain such field assignments experienced tremendous 'bonding' in the shared adversity and discomfort of their corporate puberty rites.

Puberty rites are almost always uncomfortable. Most corporate cultures conceal a few, at least for the elect, the 'A list', the chosen few. Other cultures do too; I remember a very senior doctor in one hospital who dismissed the notion that cardphones should be installed so that the 100-hour-a-week junior doctors could occasionally make personal calls. Although he was noted for his modern attitudes to management, the older doctor said: 'We had it tougher than these guys do. I don't see any reason to coddle them!'

The discomforts of puberty rites bring astronomical benefits in a sense of membership – unless it begins to be seen that no one from your cohort has had a significant promotion for the past few years. It is then possible that cohort membership can outweigh corporate culture membership, and whole groups of able people may go trailing off to the competition once one key member takes the drastic step outwards.

Rituals I used to have to help organise a ritual for STC, when the chief executive called together his top 1000 managers for an annual Saturday-morning meeting. The top team put on a glossy performance, with slides, videos, and well-rehearsed questions from the glassy-eyed audience.

I thought it was barbaric! The managers in the darkened auditorium received no useful information they didn't already have. Wives complained at the loss of a weekend. The coffee break was minuscule. No lunch was served, except to the chairman's chosen dozen. Managers winced at the very idea of going to the conference – but someone whose name was inadvertently left off the list phoned me within microseconds. No one dared miss the ritual event.

The real value of this ritual (and many others in organisational life) was the accidental meetings with old colleagues that took place during the coffee break. (My main contribution to management communication at STC was to start serving coffee at eight o'clock before the nine o'clock performance.) The corporate *cognoscenti* began arriving as early as 7.30 to see each other. The ones who liked the ritual meeting best were those from far-away plants who arrived by coach together the previous evening and stayed in hotels together, acquiring shared hangovers and less formal ritual experiences. In spite of its painful aspects, the management meeting helped reinforce the culture.

When the chief executive left, his successor's first act was to cancel the management meeting, and introduce his own rituals. Message: 'Things are going to be different around here.'

Sorcerers There is a certain amount of magic in organisations. Leaders are vested with the characteristics the culture values. Healing unguents are administered to troubled elements. Miracles take place and are recorded. The people who can most influence these phenomena are frequently not the up-front power figures.

Here the sorcerer may be the editor of the house magazine, there a management development man, somewhere else the plant manager's secretary. Generally, the sorcerer's reward is simply seeing the results of his (or her) behind-the-scenes influence. (In Belbin's terms, the sorcerers tend to be Shapers.)

Sorcery thrives in the dark. I have seen 'change agent' programmes that were counterproductive for the sorcerers, even when they were included among the elect. Culture change may be one of the phenomena where naming the agents of change out loud may be like belling the cat.

Trade Unions, Women, and Other Minorities

The way an organisation deals with 'different' people is a significant part of its culture. Young people coming fresh from school will quickly adopt the attitudes they see around them. In the past decade in the UK we have seen dramatic changes in attitudes on several fronts:

- Trade unions are decidedly more 'out'.
- Women, at least superficially, are more 'in'.

Unions and Staff Associations

These came into being because their members felt the need for someone to listen to them and speak for them. However, the union shows its worth to the members in terms of the money or other benefits it can negotiate for them – which often diverts attention from things that matter more to employees, like the long-term health of the organisation.

During the Thatcher era, when union-bashers were rewarded with knighthoods it became convenient for large organisations to denigrate their unions. But employees in large organisations will continue to feel the need for champions unless corporate behaviour changes dramatically.

A few companies have always spent a great deal of time, energy and money to remain union-free. IBM might say, very carefully, that the company has been managed in such a way that IBM employees never felt the need for collective representation. (In today's competitive computer market, IBM may actually be hampered by not understanding the real world of organisations that take union membership for granted.)

Unions bring a culture of their own, growing from questions about control of work. They built on the older models of guilds which restricted entry, controlled standards, and wielded the ultimate sanction of depriving members of their livelihood if they did not live up to group norms. Just as companies belong to their shareholders and owners, so unions belong to their members. The union is based on the inverted pyramid. Ultimately, the members tell the General Secretary what to do (not vice versa, as one or two have thought for a while), and they pay his (or her) salary directly.

The two systems ought to fit together into a diamond shape. They have the same people in common. The organisation needs the people to keep working so that it can achieve its task. The union representatives and officials those people have elected need the company to go on working, so that the members can remain employed.

How the organisation deals with its unions is an important element of its culture. Many with cautious cultures keep 'owner-ship' of industrial relations in the personnel function – which gives more power, *de facto*, to the reps on the line, who are able to bypass line management more easily, and go straight to the chairman as they please.

The unions know that they survive on their communication skills, though managers don't always recognise this. Hearts and minds – both depend on obtaining information and believing it. Some organisations leave it to the union representatives to tell people on the front line what is happening, but ceding communication does not help their employees. Management loses 'control' or even access to the hearts and minds of their people; furthermore, members grow cynical, seeing the 'union bosses' as just another boss class.

Women, the Invisible Force

What man has been asked in a job interview about his child-care arrangements? Women are still an under-used resource, but their importance to organisations is growing. In Sweden 82 per cent of women work; in the USA it is about 77 per cent; in the UK 67 per cent – and growing everywhere.

Women's own attitudes are part of this culture, and obstacles to their advancement. Strident demands for crèches are not always helpful. Most women believe their employers would not spend on them thousands of pounds on management courses that are quite standard for male colleagues. A few prefer not to accept responsibilities that might interfere with traditional demands. I know a factory in Wales where at least a dozen very able female supervisors have to leave promptly at 4.30 to go home and make a meal for their families; the factory manager promoted them without demanding evening work.

Women perceive 'glass ceilings' – invisible but real barriers to advancement. A few organisations, especially those with civil service roots, have strict and fair routes for advancement, at least through the first pane of glass. That may help to explain why BT has many more women in senior management positions than even IBM.

Women can enrich the competence of an organisation. On any course with a female presence, everyone learns more. A committee that includes women (at least one-third) has different processes:

- discussion is more 'wholistic';
- issues discussed reflect the constituencies better;
- members understand better how conclusions are reached.

According to recent research, women tend to understand what makes people tick, and those skills are increasingly needed in organisations trying to shift from power and control towards networks, co-operation, and empowered employees.

Women are good at sharing information as well as power. Once they reach positions at the top, they try to create flexible organisations. They are interested in individuals, not just hierarchies.

One personnel director admitted recently: 'They're cheaper, they work harder, and they do better work.' They also tend to be more faithful and stay in their jobs longer, even to their own detriment.

In addition, women are better than men at finding ways to help everyone win. The young men and women who experience this kind of leadership in today's cultures may be able to develop better paradigms for the organisations of tomorrow.

The Strongest Signs are Non-verbal

The organisation does not own its culture, but you can map it . . . or bend it a little . . . . . . or heighten and highlight it. By behaving consistently over the long term, management can help create or change a culture. The real trick is making sure people's perceptions match the management claims. The moment they diverge, the perceptions always win.

Most organisations these days are trying to increase involvement and empowerment. They have seen the outer limits of systems, automation, assembly lines, and realise that the leaner, more flexible organisations they want depend much more on the abilities of their people.

But such changes in culture are vulnerable to knee-jerk reflexes – management responses to a thousand large and small stimuli. Only if management behaves in a way that is truly consistent with its claims can it influence the culture. A single lapse or exception can convince people that the old ways still prevail after all.

Consistency means that every member gets the message, that the formal and informal messages match. A good grapevine is an opportunity, not a threat. Make sure that the formal communications match it, and that people can trust their formal sources, particularly credible front-line management. If there is a gap, the grapevine wins – and culture change loses.

As I mentioned before, the quickest way to change the culture is to fire a well-known baddie – and make sure everyone knows (informally) why he was fired. When someone leaves an organisation suddenly, people generally assume the worst. Management usually tells ritual lies: 'He has submitted his resignation for personal reasons' is polite, but leaves people wide latitude to invent a thousand 'real reasons'.

If the victim is able to explain his own departure honestly, he may reinforce or restructure cultural values: 'The chairman wants to put more emphasis on marketing, so he'll need someone with a different outlook in my place.'

The management that recognises the overt and hidden values within its own culture can reinforce them, or plan ways to shift them, gradually, by making new heroes, encouraging new myths, abetting new sorcerers, redeeming sinners in different ways.

8

Bridging the Hypocrisy Gap

Empowering people is not going to change human nature. Nor should it. Empowering will only work when it condones, lives with, even celebrates human nature – including the scepticism, on days and off days, and the normal foibles with which we all embroider ourselves. But empowered people who feel sceptical feel free to say so, and really manageable organisations that want to empower them will try not to enforce too much lip service.

Cynics are made, not born. Left to fester, their cynicism works against empowerment for their colleagues. The sooner an organisation recognises that they are entitled to their cynical views the sooner it can tackle the causes rather than the attitudes.

This chapter deals with the way people feel in large organisations when they see managers changing their tunes too quickly, or espousing less-than-credible top-down claims too enthusiastically. Especially in communicating strategy, actions speak louder than words.[1]

No Time for Ambivalence

Most large organisations are going through a period of tremendous tension. Many need to slim down to remain competitive. This causes an organisational 'ambivalence': at the same time as they are downsizing, letting go long-term, loyal employees, they are also trying to achieve the open, trusting, flexible, communicating, empowering, people-oriented culture we all say is necessary for their future survival.

The word 'ambivalence' comes from the Latin *ambo* (both) and *valere* (to be strong). Psychologists use the term to describe people suffering stress as a result of simultaneous or alternating attitudes, feelings, or values. If you are writing fiction, ambivalence is considered A Good Thing – your writing will be commended for its strength and tension, your ambivalent character will be hailed as 'subtle'.

On the other hand, if you are a manager, ambivalence is usually outlawed. Most organisations demand instant acceptance of any decision, adherence to any new party line; the higher you go up the tree, the more aware you are of the miasma of 'loyalty' and 'obedience' expected of you – and the brighter you are, the more likely you are to perceive how little of the breadth of your brightness is wanted. Just focus the bits that fit and ignore the rest.

That is as it is, and probably always will be to some extent. Managers suffer more stress as they see their roles changing too fast for comfort. If they have time to reflect, they see themselves torn between self-images that are soft and hard, systems that are open and closed, caught between management art and management science. It is the age-old tension between yin and yang, female and male.

There should be energy in this tension; it comes from a real shift away from masculine yang and towards more feminine yin in organisational behaviour. But in most organisations, people (especially managers) have to waste a great deal of energy in damping down the tension, hiding ambivalence rather than confronting and using it.

Hierarchy Inhales Information

The very managers who say they want to launch change programmes in your organisation got where they are today through the old culture – closed, game-playing, macho, power-broking, controlling, hierarchical, deferential, bureaucratic.

In my experience most large organisations are trying to escape from this kind of culture, which is a natural result of size. In such a culture information is hoovered into the centre. Decisions are announced, but the real reasons behind them are only whispered, if they are communicated at all.

In one large company, a new manager asked someone in Personnel how they scheduled appraisals. 'We'll get back to you,' they said. Five weeks later he received a ten-page questionnaire, demanding response yesterday, all about how he went about scheduling his appraisals. He phoned up, irate: 'This is in response to my question last month – and I've long since asked other managers myself.' Personnel explained blandly that they were now embarked on the research, so he had better fill out the form.

Is it any wonder that managers should be in two minds about change! Yet their world displays little tolerance for their ambivalence. To express conflicting feelings would be confusing, seen as indecisive, a sign of weakness or conflicting loyalty, or a sign of flagging commitment – in organisations that set great store by commitment.

Loyalty Cuts Both Ways

Loyalty is a two-edged sword. The organisation that expects loyalty from its employees, particularly managers, must make sure they see it being loyal in return. If they perceive an imbalance they doubt much of what the organisation tries to tell them.

Good managers can usually see both sides (more often every side) of a question; good managers can also take decisions in spite of incomplete information. Yet the moment a key decision is made, most organisations expect every manager to support it with noisy wholeheartedness. There is no time to mourn the demise of the other approach you were supporting, or explore and understand the reasons behind the decision. You are expected to just stay in line and cheer.

I contend that the organisation would do better if it took a more literary view of ambivalence – encouraging the good managers who are strong enough to admit their own ability to see several ways at once. Respecting and licensing their ambivalence is likely to result in more and better information for future decisions, as well as less lip service and lower leakage of good managers.

Hypocrisy Thrives in the Dark

It upsets people to look up and see leaders they want to respect turning emotional somersaults as they join up to salute the new party line. In his own eyes, and those of his subordinates, a manager who has to pretend enthusiasm while he is still full of doubts is being hypocritical.

The hypocrite is lying to people (and ultimately to himself) in pretending to be more certain than he is. The ambivalent manager may see himself simply trying to suppress some lingering doubts. From below, however, he looks like deceitful and two-faced. His credibility slips as his people stop trusting his judgement and honesty if he lies both to them and himself.

If the manager tells his subordinates the truth – that he does not really support the current line – he keeps credibility below, but his people see him kowtowing to something they know he does not believe in, and the divergence makes him vulnerable to those above.

Instances of hypocrisy will occur as long as there are humans to create and perceive them – but they can be made fewer and smaller.

Hypocrisy may be an organisational accident. Most organisations contain 'amplifiers' – people who pick up a whim from the chief and expand it into a commandment for the multitudes. IBM's Thomas Watson Jr once told me: 'When I sneeze, the Dallas office explodes.' Everyone treats the chief with rapidly responsive, unquestioning reverence. Careful executives have to learn to muffle their asides, and to deploy their attention along a few carefully chosen lines – but this deadly deference actually harms the chief as well as his organisation!

The formal communication system moves in behind a decision, inexorably claiming too much, painting the future too perfectly. I helped to start some quality circles that worked quite well, only to see them falter when their members read the exaggerated nonsense that the company paper saw fit to print about them. In one case it was my own fault; a group was so proud of the project they had launched, which had saved the company over £50,000, that I invited the editor of the company paper in. He publicised the project well, but the group never met again. When I met one member later he explained: 'We couldn't find any more projects that would save £50,000, so we gave up.' No paper-chase, no coffee-machine debate, no clean-up campaign, no team spirit. Nothing. Just a one-shot project.

What I am really talking about is the underpinning to credibility and trust. These phenomena do not belong to the manager but to the managed. Credibility and trust do not move in straight, manageable lines. They race along under their own momentum until they go over a cliff, freewheeling madly for a moment, then plummeting down. Building them up again is a long, slow process.

The only way to build trust is to take risks and expose yourself. That is difficult at any time, but especially hard to do when you are new – that is when you tend to be most cautious about speaking your mind. You would like to be open, to have a free zone where you can express your feelings and frustrations, but you do not yet know who to trust, or how people behave in your new environment. Your subordinates, eager for signs of your style, see pretence where you intended only silence. They quickly let go of their hopes and turn away, disappointed. If this happens you become less effective, but it is difficult to understand why.

The Cynic-making Machinery

A cynic is one who questions the sincerity and goodness of

people. The Greeks once spawned a prickly set of philosophers called 'cynics' who regarded virtue as the supreme good and despised all comfort (the word comes from the Greek for 'dog-like' – they led dogs' lives!). They are remembered more today for their disbelief than for the idealism that lurked beneath it.

In a large organisation it is easy to find the cynics. They glance at each other when ambitious announcements are made. They make irreverent remarks when the company newspaper arrives. They can tell a thousand stories of Great Change Programmes or New Projects that came to naught. Like frigid wives, they gave up hoping long ago, and have channelled their energy into covering up their nerve endings, diverting their efforts into more amusing pursuits, or more fruitful outside activities.

The cynic, without lifting a hand, can stop good things from happening.

These people are entitled to be cynics! They are capable of visualising a more perfect world. They see all the small, tawdry acts by which the organisation itself (or its managers) expresses its ambivalence.

One company recently put together an exceptionally generous package to entice its members to apply for early retirement. People murmured approvingly to each other, and began to do sums on the backs of envelopes – until they started hearing tales of older colleagues, people who had been there for 30 or 40 years, who were given only two or three days to make a choice that would affect the rest of their lives. The entire programme silently curdled. The cynics said to each other: 'See, we were right. The company doesn't really care about its people.'

Management in that company may have had reasons for the rush and the secrecy – but the topic was never discussed openly. People taking golden handshakes slunk out with minimum ceremony. No thanks, no goodbye, no party. The cynics thrived – cynicism does thrive, where management says least.

Gap Management

Every physics student knows there is energy in gaps. You can see it in those experiments where two live wires are held a little distance apart and a brilliant spark leaps across. Hold them too far apart, though, and nothing happens. Worse, if you have an audience expecting a spark and you cannot produce one, you lose credibility. The trick is to know how big a gap your spark can leap. To achieve real change you often have to stretch a little, to set targets that are ambitious but not impossible.

The cynic's energy comes from the 'hypocrisy gap', the yawning chasm between what is, what is claimed, and what the cynic once wished would be. The ability to visualise an ideal world is shared by the cynic and the organisational change agent.

- The cynic sees the gap between reality and claim as unbridgeable.
- The change agent believes it can be bridged.

Part of this is in the seeing, and part of it is in the distance to the vision. The cynic, with more idealism than average, already has a natural tendency to place his own vision a long way out towards perfection. When the organisation connives in this and even exceeds the distance, it reinforces his cynicism, and loses the chance to enlist his (or her) energy, because the gap between the claim and the vision is impossible to bridge.

The change agent has to be an optimist – but a practical optimist who can be content with smaller steps, with more manageable vision. The organisation that recognises and supports this incremental view towards change has a better chance of achieving it.

There is exhilaration in reaching for tough goals. Energy is reinforced when people meet them and are recognised for it. Soggy, easily achieved goals never do much for anybody (certainly not the cynics). But panicky, unachievable goals do even less, especially if they are buttressed by fear.

As we have already noted, the Japanese have been perfectly willing to share their mastery of the gap between what is, and what is claimed. They do not count on the sensational announcement, or publication of the new organisation chart, to trigger new relationships. They try things, little by little, until the new organisation they want has evolved.

These days, with so many organisations shrinking actively or passively, the danger of creating incredible gaps is increasing. I know one factory in South Wales where the manager was enthusiastic about the team briefing programme that headquarters was promoting. He held several inspirational meetings and put his own credibility behind the briefings: 'You'll hear it from me first.' Supervisors were trained. The management team attended seminars. The briefings began, and ideas began to flow, too.

Then one day the manager had a phone call from the local paper. 'We hear the company is letting 30 people go from your factory.' When the smoke cleared, his embarrassed boss explained: 'Yes, we were trying to phone you last night to tell you.' He had never been involved, nor even consulted in the decision.

The enthusiastic manager turned off, settled back and marked time (competently) for 12 more years before he could take early retirement. His people's expertise and ideas remained untapped for the whole of that time. The company never measured the value of 12 years of his commitment or his people's ideas.

Redemption?

No wonder God so loved sinners: they make such splendid examples when they reform!

You can't change human nature, and you needn't. We have ample evidence that the same person can be a villain in one setting and a hero in another. Sometimes the difference is the (Belbin-described) mix of people in a team. Sometimes it is a bit of missing machinery.

One abysmal manager in a service organisation played his cards too close to his chest and deployed his dozen professional people with too-small assignments (often overlapping or conflicting). He became a hero in their eyes when he gave in to their demands and started having a 20-minute meeting every Monday to review their work. He had not changed his personality. He remained simply a pleasant but abysmal manager and terrible delegator who now has a Monday meeting with a good set of people who keep him (and each other) better informed.

The key to unravelling the vicious circle of ambivalence, hypocrisy, and cynicism is to open it up, to let in the air, to license things as they actually are.

In summary, here are a few observations that may be useful to managers who are genuinely trying to change their organisations for the better:

- People involved in conflict and competition are entitled to be ambivalent as projects are developed and resolved.
- They can help most if they are able to express their ambivalence. This often requires special structures or mechanisms (for example, a Chinese Wall, or a very open house journal) to make ambivalence acceptable.
- It takes time before people can develop commitment to the new direction.
- The less publicity your goodnesses receive, the more chance they have to become real.
- Employees are entitled to feel cynical.
- Cynical feelings are long lasting. Driven underground, they can fester for many years after the events that triggered them.
- Cynics who have a chance to express themselves fully have the best chance of being turned into agents of change.
- The difference between the cynic and the change agent is often the size of the gap between the reality and the vision.
- Only long, slow, 'reasons why', 'warts-and-all' communication will change existing cynics or prevent the creation of new ones.

Nobody said it was easy, but the cynics' bark can be worse than their bite – and even the barking stops when a cynic realises that what appeared from below to be hypocrisy was only an inevitable (and very human) ambivalence.

Note

1. Some of the material in this chapter first appeared in *New Management* (Los Angeles), Vol. 2, No. 4, Spring 1985.

9

Delayering and Downsizing

Delayering, downsizing, rationalising and restructuring are an inherent dark shadow to most empowerment drives today.

It may be too simplistic to say merely that the number of layers takes power away from people. Layers are artifacts, invented to protect managers from problems, or to evade restrictions in formal pay systems: 'We can give Harold a rise if he is described as George's boss.' Once they are invented, layers tend to harden into rock-like structures. The disempowering effect comes not just from the existence of layers but from people's feeling that change is impossible because of the unholy combination of blaming, culture, impenetrable layers and structure.

Slimming Gradually

To empower people, these layers need to be eroded, gradually, together, with everyone knowing what is going on, and why. Delayering alone leaves you with a flatter bureaucracy, no more empowered, but with a number of people afraid that their own layer comes next.

Delayering works best when it is planned nearest the face – a form of subsidiarity. If you shift the organisation style towards something like *primus inter pares* (first among equals) at the front line, you may be able to push two layers together. Volvo achieved this, over a period of years, at considerable trouble and expense. The whole approach to work changed, with assembly lines giving way to rather autonomous groups, while the systems brought supplies to the groups just in time. They monitored their own quality, and Volvo survives today because of these changes in the 1970s. Volvo eliminated several layers of management, and changed many of the tough 'father' supervisors ('yang' style) into more maternal ('yin') style training and coaching supervisors – with no loss of status.

The layers in the middle of the organisation, the ones that most need rationalising, are clearly best at self-preservation, and it often takes strong pincers between the bottom and the top to delayer effectively. Delayering can never really be a voluntary activity. People will rarely co-operate in their own elimination.

I do not like the American term 'downsizing' any more than I like the phenomenon itself, but it is a fact of life. If it has to be done, it can be done better or worse – and better is better.

The American Research

A Philadelphia consultancy called Right Associates did some research in the US that raised doubts about whether cutting staff numbers actually achieves what organisations expect. They surveyed 1024 American companies, of which about 75 per cent said they had downsized – sacked 500 employees or more – during the previous five years. (This is considerably easier in the US than it is in Europe – the employee usually just gets his notice (a pink slip) and two weeks' pay.)

One would expect financial performance and productivity to rise, but this was not so. Only a third said they saw any improvement in productivity, and only a quarter said their financial performance had improved.

There seemed a close correlation with employee communications. Only 18 per cent of the firms surveyed had explained to their workers how the cut in jobs fitted into future plans. Most of the employees who kept their jobs felt insecure. Morale plummeted. Managers seemed surprised to discover that increased productivity is hard to extract from a population of turtles who have disappeared inside their shells.

It is difficult to tell people why you are downsizing, when you are not sure yourself. Less than half the companies Right Associates surveyed saw their job cuts as part of a wider strategy – they just thought it would make them more competitive. *The Economist* put it bluntly:[1] 'If you merely downsize GM, the result may be a smaller GM, with all the problems it had when it was bigger.' In other words, you only get 'more with less' when you know what you are doing, and why – and when you communicate this credibly and effectively to the entire workforce.

Communication and Security

Most firms do not like to talk about unpleasant subjects like letting their workers go. Managers find out that cuts are coming, but each tries to fight for his own section; 'As long as you don't have any announcements, there's a better chance you might save a few jobs.' That is one rationale I hear quite frequently while they talk about 'security', in the secret service sense of the word.

My own suspicion is that managers simply don't like having to go out and talk to their people when they don't have all the answers. They find excuses to keep the impending changes under wraps, because someone is likely to ask: 'But what about *me*?'

The best military commanders wait until they have enough ammunition to win before they go in to attack. Managers often believe they should wait until they are fully armed. But infor- · mation is the most volatile ammunition of all. It is impossible to stockpile information. It can leak. It rapidly passes its 'use-by' date. It can explode.

The absence of management communication is not the absence of all communication. By the time the management infighting is in full swing, most employees have heard their own rumbles on the grapevine. In the absence of clear information, every individual assumes the worst for himself. That seems to be human nature.

Remember Maslow's needs? No sooner is a newborn infant fed than he moves up the hierarchy to worry whether he is going to be fed again in three hours. The name for that need is 'security', in the human sense of the word. It is very difficult to go on to higher needs when everyone is starved of security. That is what happens throughout the organisation when job cuts impend for a long time without becoming clear.

How Sweet the Pot?

There are various ways to talk to employees when downsizing impends. My favourite goes something along these lines:

> Hello. This is your chairman speaking. You all know we've been having difficult times in our company because the competition is fierce, and our costs are higher than others'. The board has decided we need to learn how to operate with more output and fewer people. The fairest way to slim down is to offer voluntary severance or early retirement to any employee who wants it. We're offering an extra £xxxx for every year you've been with us, plus your normal entitlements to pension, with one month's notice. We'll pay for any reasonable retraining you want, for up to six months. I myself plan to retrain for Voluntary Service Overseas.
>
> Anyone who wants this offer is entitled to have it, but for some of you we ask that you spend an extra few weeks helping someone else learn how you do your job, and perhaps helping us to organise it more efficiently. Each of you is the real expert on how your job works. We'll pay you on a consultancy basis for that help. This offer will remain open for three months, and then we'll review the situation and let you know how we're progressing. Your own manager will have up-to-date information on your current entitlement.

John Akers did something like this when he resigned as IBM's chairman in early 1993. Some kind of absolutely open offer, one which allows everyone to calculate his or her own entitlement, seems the fairest first step to reducing a workforce.

The pot probably has to be sweetened. If it is sweetened too selectively, or over-sweetened, you have to tell people they cannot go – after they have gone through the emotional upheaval of reviewing their lives and taking steps towards this very serious decision. You may not lose their bodies, but the warmth and soul have evaporated.

If the pot is sweetened too little, the organisation will know soon enough: too few will take up the offer. It is always possible to add a little more (as long as you are willing to recompense the few pioneers as well – fairness is important in the eyes of employees). It is impossible to take some of the sweeteners away once you have announced them.

In Part III of this book, we look at employee communications in BT and IBM. It is no coincidence that when 30,000 miners were to go, people took to the streets in protest – but when BT let almost 20,000 go on a single day, probably with similar-sized payoffs, there was hardly a murmur: BT had invested a few years in building management credibility. People understood why it was happening, and to some extent they felt they had choices, that it was voluntary.

With IBM the number worldwide in 1992 was 40,000, with at least 25,000 more scheduled to go in 1993. The company was trying to maintain the voluntary nature of the exercise in the face of dire losses, but the press was more interested in the IBM story, mainly in 'How the mighty have fallen' mode. In an era of disappearing jobs, it may be more useful to explore these cases to see how major job-losses have been handled so that those remaining have a workable vision of where they are going and how they are going to get there.

Who Goes? Who Stays?

Many organisations feel insecure in making any kind of offer to all employees. They are concerned, quite rightly, that they might lose their best people, and so they might. But if they do not make an open offer to all employees, those best people, who are probably best tuned into the grapevine, will already have their CVs polished up, and can be found perusing the trade press or fat Sunday paper situations vacant advertisements. It is usually the ablest who leave first. The ones who work because it is fun, because they like to win, will go somewhere where there is a better chance to win, once the gloom starts to spread.

It is quite normal and natural to want to go out with a rifle and eliminate all the dross, while keeping the best people, but I do not think it works. If an organisation has dross, those people were probably quite normal when they started. They have been left to moulder with poor policies or poor management. Getting rid of them will not improve the organisation; the rifle approach harms the best people, harms the normal people, misses plenty of dross, and harms the organisation.

Many companies have taken the age-related route. In the past ten years I have seen the *de facto* retirement age in large organisations go from 65 to 55. These days it's hard to find anyone over 50 in ICI or IBM or NatWest. It was difficult for the pioneering companies at first, it is much easier now.

The pioneers spent years planting good people in outside secondments, encouraging them to take peripheral parts of the business outside and start their own firms, generally developing them and encouraging a spirit of enterprise that thrives on smallness. ICI in particular took a conscious decision to move in this direction at least 15 years ago, and has had excellent managers running the programme through the years, to everyone's benefit.

Where unions are involved and redundancy is compulsory, there is usually a 'last in, first out' approach. It may seem fair to those who value loyalty, but there must be a better way! An organisation that needs to slim has got itself in trouble. Retaining the older employees, insecure and frozen into the traditional ways of doing things, is not the best approach to the innovation that is needed. How did they become like that?

The evidence suggests that, after decades of formal management 'development', most large organisations have become better and better at management destruction. Courses build culture and loyalty and language and networks, but underneath they are dis-empowering managers, eroding confidence in their own judgement and trying to replace it with faith in 'systems'. If this is so, you might as well get rid of the older managers first.

You do not have to overprotect people who have become a burden. The blocking bureaucrat can be moved sideways, even demoted, and a healthy message goes out into the organisation. Many people will think again about 'taking the offer' if their status is about to be visibly reduced. But the decision should still be on their own shoulders, not the organisation's.

I am convinced that 'voluntary' is the key to downsizing. Respect for people at work means giving them full information, the moment it is possible, and letting it percolate through each person's thinking, at his or her own speed. People react at different rates, so a longer-term programme will work best. Some will go rapidly, and others will only consider it when they see former workmates enjoying a new situation.

Taking Care of Those Who Go

The organisation needs to be concerned about the *welfare* of those who go, and about *empowering* those who stay. Taking good care of the employees who go is not only a matter of decency; it also sends important messages to those who stay:

- No need to feel guilty about surviving; those who went were well taken care of.
- We value our employees, even when they go.
- You, too, may make this choice someday. You will not suffer if you do.
- Those of us who are left have to work in new ways.

Leaving an organisation where you have spent some significant portion of your life is a wrench. Younger people taking up an open offer usually have some kind of plan to change careers. For people approaching retirement age, the change to non-work can be downright dangerous. (It used to be said that Ford had the fattest pension fund around because so many Ford people worked pell-mell till the day they retired, then died within nine months.) Look at the changes:

- What do you do with your time?
- Who wants your skills?
- Where do you eat lunch?

- What do you say when people ask: 'What do you do?'
- How do you make ends meet?

Very few pre-retirement programmes deal with these kinds of questions. They concern themselves more with health and legal issues. I would contend that newly retired people can grow rapidly older and less healthy simply because these 'identity' questions are unanswered. You do not acquire 'identity' from playing golf, decorating the loo, or going shopping with your wife. I worry most about those just too old to start new careers, and just too young to accept 'non-identity'. Early retirement has dramatically enlarged this category.

A few companies have 'soft-landing' approaches, with secondments or part-time work in the community for people in their last few years of work. Some have days when pensioners are welcomed back to the canteen. A few have pensioner clubs which keep up some semblance of social contact and welfare visiting. All these are useful, not only to the pensioners, but to the remaining workforce.

The Open Learning programmes that are starting in some large organisations may help people explore alternative interests before leisure is forced on them (or they take it on themselves) in unmanageably large chunks.

'More with Less' – Achieving Productivity Objectives

Derek Sheane[2] identified the normal causes of middle management overload:

- Too many people to communicate with in order to influence.
- Too many meetings to attend.
- Too much travel.
- Too little space between events.

In most organisations today, the downsizing exercise takes so much energy that no one has time to really plan for what happens afterwards. So the overworked middle managers who survive find themselves doing more of the donkey-work that their newly retired junior colleagues used to do. The combination of 'normal' industrial overload and overwhelming demands for change from every direction often causes managers to resist or block anything but routine. Their skills at surviving take over, and their coping mechanisms force them to freeze. That certainly works against any empowerment for anyone below them –just at the time that those above them are talking more about empowerment.

Those managers need space and time to adapt and begin to create the new environment that is wanted. Overload has to be lifted. In place of hurried meetings all over the country, this may be the time to take them away in residential clusters to plan the transition and support each other as they build new networks.

It is often said that there are two occasions when you can achieve real change in an organisation:

- When things are so good it can't hurt to try; and
- When things are so bad they can't get any worse.

Pulling a company back from the abyss, takes a particularly robust, open kind of management, right from the top. The first step into the new environment must be to *make the objectives crystal clear*. Then find some way for every employee who stays to look at his job in terms of those objectives – for the organisation and for the group.

- This is where we have been –
- and this is where we are going –
- and this is how we are going to get there.

This is the time for positive team-building activities. Not 'Team Building Training' – heaven forbid! That is one of the terms (like 'marriage guidance') that becomes counterproductive the moment it is uttered. Positive activities for streamlined teams immediately after an organisation has downsized would be setting tasks and achieving them.

This is the time to build teams across walls in the organisation. Marketing and Production have never worked together very well. Instead of haranguing about it, analysing the past to death, put some key people from both divisions into a room with some Design people, and talk about the next generation of products. Keep talking. Form subgroups. Look at tasks, not roles.

This is the time to explore those measures of success: more projects; specifying standards which can be met; making sure that they are monitored and that success is recognised.

If downsizing has been truly voluntary, then those who stayed were making a real commitment to the organisation. 'I could have gone; I would have done very well; but I love my job, and I think this company is going places now.' That is how the employees should feel. That gives an organisation tremendous momentum if people's commitment can be focused on performance, and they feel empowered and involved.

There may come a time when a few organisations, blessed with brilliant manpower planning and understanding of technology advances, may choose to make downsizing a continuing process, part of the culture. The human body, as it grows older sheds more cells than it generates. Similarly, an organisation might regenerate 'lean', to make sure there is always room to bring in new energy. In that context, there would be no need to 'get it over with quickly'. People coming in would understand their 'sell-by dates' with plenty of time to plan for the next phase in their lives.

But for the time being, in ordinary organisations, if downsizing is necessary, then certainly get it over with quickly. Job uncertainty is depressing, to individuals as well as economies; none of us can afford depression. There is too much to be done!

Notes

1. 'Pink-slip productivity', *The Economist*, 28 March 1992.

2. Derek Sheane (1976), *Beyond Bureaucracy*, Bolton, Lancs.: Management Research.

10

Don't Disempower the Middle!

What is the opposite of 'empowering'? It must be somewhere between 'castrating' and 'enmeshing'. Rationalise the middle, if it is silted up, but for goodness' sake, don't disempower it. You need it to bring about change.

Blaming Creates Layers

The head of a large Scottish organisation recently held a meeting with a group of his key executives, many of them new after a massive reorganisation. After he had expostulated passionately about the grand strategy, one of the managers bravely asked: 'What do you expect of us?' The answer came back instantly: 'No cock-ups!' With that one phrase he had put back the clock. No one was going to venture into anything new unless it was absolutely certain that all cock-ups could be avoided. That is not the nature of change.

The top in a large organisation is a long way from practical reality. Heating engineers, grannies, complacent board members all know that the more layers you have, the cosier you feel (so do hierarchy climbers, degree collectors, and status seekers). All those layers insulate the top from the front line, and vice versa. The layers tend to be created when blaming sets in. Many less-complacent board members feel cut off by the layers, and want to be nearer the action.

The more management layers an organisation has created in its middle, the more likely it is that those who created the layers believe that the top should be protected from direct information from the bottom.

Layers are created by people who believe that the *mechanics* of organisation (the layers depicted on the chart) can work without the *electronics* (the rich mix of formal and informal communication links up, down and across the formal structure).

Counter-productivity

Added layers make it easier to create 'managers' who help to absolve colleagues from specific responsibilities. In some organisations, I am concerned that the creation of a Communication Manager will help absolve all others from having to bother about communication.

Layer-creating has certainly gone too far, and most large organisations know it. The people at the top are trying to change it now, though I do not think most of them are going about it the most effective way. The temptation for people on high to tinker with the organisation chart is seductive. Britain is just emerging from a disastrous period of chairman-initiated top-down re-organisations, which tend to be blessed with trendy (sometimes counterproductive) names – for example:

- In BT it was 'Project Sovereign', when they went from geographical to functional, splitting into 'personal' and 'business' sectors.
- British Rail called it 'Organising For Quality' (alias 'O for Q'), and pushed further down the line into accountable 'businesses', until rail privatisation cut across all its progress.
- British Gas had 'Regional Organisation Review' (alias 'ROR'),

and went more geographical, from strong regions towards scrappy little districts.

Many others are similarly in process, often accompanied by early retirement for managers, and general uncertainty for most employees for an unconscionable period.

Real change, in positive directions that are good for the long-term future of the organisation, is impossible when people are scared, insecure, overloaded, stressed – and all these are the consequences of top-down reorganising.

By the very nature of size, once the top has announced that change is imminent, it is slowed. The chairman believes everyone will be in post by next July, and assumes his own top team will be in place by May. He fails to realize that (*a*) at least one top-team candidate will stop to bargain; (*b*) another would prefer not to be sent out into the field; and (*c*) the same delays will occur at six additional once-cosy levels in the organisation before things settle down and people can get back to work.

It is the managers in the middle who are making those 'new' organisations work, no matter how horrific the process, minus a middle layer or two and a lot of useful troops.

Middle Managers – Filters, Felt, Fire-fighters?

Viewed from the middle, the top seems prone to management by slogan; they talk about change, and create infinite opportunities for cynicism, while the real managers have to keep quiet and do the changing. Miraculously, managers in the middle often manage.

The managers in the middle learn to be filters. Even without the added impetus of the chairman's reorganisation, so much bumf emanates from the top of the typical large organisation that overworked managers have to filter out the boring bits, or the vast quantity of communications and procedures, 'processes', and general orders that simply are not relevant.

Then, as the managers grow older and wiser, especially in an environment where blame may be apportioned rather easily, they learn to filter out the gritty bits from the meagre communications their people try to push upward. (The better the managers become at this upward filtering, the more employees have to go around them via union representatives.)

In most large organisations, these days, the middle management filter layers are like raw wool: what started as a wholesome natural white, fluffy, useful material becomes agitated; it spends too much time in hot water, and it comes out like felt: solid, matted down, impenetrable. In a blaming culture, nothing finds its way through the felted layers of management in either direction.

This is not necessarily the fault of the managers. In the beginning they were probably innocent, eager, even passionate, full of idealism and desire to make things much better. The fault lies in the intrinsic, amplifying nature of large organisations – indrawn breath: 'Oh, I don't think you ought to put it that way!' or 'We do things differently in this company.'

A few people are natural inward–upward managers (also known as in-house politicians). These thrive by giving upstairs whatever it wants, and trying not to notice messages from below that do not fit the pattern. (The opposite type, the downward–outward manager, is much better to work for, but does not always get the resources to achieve the task, given the arcane nature of the large organisation.)

Even for the most open, positive, people-oriented down-and-out manager, fire-fighting takes up the time that ought to be spent on managing. After a major reorganisation most upper-middle managers find their lives full of lower-middle management tasks nobody realised would fall between stools. The filters lose buffers.

Many managers would like to empower their people. (Ask them; most will say, yes, and they wouldn't mind if their bosses felt likewise.) They would even like to keep their people informed. They are simply so busy fighting all those fires they forget to delegate or communicate. The team goes without a meeting; the focus becomes fuzzy.

'It's all these interruptions,' the manager explains.

A classic study by Henry Minzberg[1] showed what managers actually do (as opposed to what they think they do). For most, the 'interruptions' are the real job. What they think is being inter-rupted (usually paperwork) is not nearly as relevant to the task. If things are so peaceful that the manager can actually get all his paperwork under control, either the organisation is moribund or he is not out walking the job as he should. Managing takes place on the landings; decisions are made in loos; information moves around the floor on foot, not on paper – not even on screen.

So the typical fire-fighting manager, with good intentions, needs some structures to underpin his desire to empower his people. Structures? A Monday-morning team meeting; or leaving ten minutes earlier on the way to lunch, to browse through the department asking specific questions about performance (one manager calls this his 'asking and thanking time'). Quality Improvement Teams and other modern management methods are full of little rules and gimmicks that actually help managers do what they want to do – empower their people.

Change Comes from the Middle

There are plenty of good managers in the middle, coping. Some of the best become invisible. A few use that invisibility to help make things happen. It gives them great satisfaction to help other people win. They know where all the bodies are buried, and where the pitfalls are, and they can tiptoe around obstructions and encourage change. They are the ones who can do most to empower the front line when conditions are right.

Genuine change in complex organisations often comes from the middle – the professionals near enough to the face to know what is possible, what is going on, where the levers of change are – and near enough to the top to put the right aspect on local initiatives and protect them until they are rooted.

Three American professors[2] spent four years studying organisational change in six companies. They said: 'The greatest obstacle to revitalization is the idea that it comes about through company-wide change programs, particularly when a corporate staff group such as human resources sponsors them.' The changes that worked did not focus on relationships or culture or sheep-dip training. They came from *ad hoc* arrangements to solve actual business problems. Aligning roles, responsibilities and relationships to deal with the task, local managers were able to develop workable change processes: We believe that an approach to change based on task alignment, starting at the periphery and moving steadily toward the corporate core, is the most effective way to achieve enduring organizational change.' The professors point out that it is a rare chief executive who knows all the details of organisational change that the many diverse units of a large corporation need. Furthermore, most chief executives developed in the era of top-down hierarchies. 'They must learn from innovative approaches coming from younger unit managers closer to the action.'

The fallacy the professors found ('the fallacy of programmatic change') is the all-too-prevalent notion that you begin with the knowledge and attitudes of individuals – the 'sheep-dip' approach. Put everyone through the same sheep-dip seminars, and out they will come with changed attitudes, leading to new behaviour, in unison.

In reality, the best way to change behaviour is to put people into a new organisation, which imposes new roles, responsibilities and relationships. The situation then 'forces' new attitudes and behaviours – they perform well, they like winning, they look for more and better ways to win. Change grows organically, from seeds. They identified certain prerequisites for corporate revitalisation:

- *teamwork* – close co-ordination among departments, as well as between managers and workers.
- *commitment* – the workers and managers needed high commitment to persevere with the initiative, co-operation, and sheer effort their coordinated action required.
- *skills and knowledge* – including knowledge of the business as a whole, analytical skill, and interpersonal skill.

Most top-down change programmes deal with one or two of these factors, but all three are essential. Without *real* teamwork and co-ordination, a grand statement about co-operation is worse than meaningless. The professors noted a tendency for the chief executive to try another programme when the first one-size-fits-all fails:

Buzzwords like 'quality', 'participation', 'excellence', 'empower-

ment', and 'leadership' become a substitute for a detailed understanding of the business. . . . By promoting skepticism and
cynicism, programmatic change can inoculate companies against
the real thing.

Exploring some of the organisations which had succeeded, using
the task approach, the professors catalogued six basic steps:

1. Mobilise commitment to change through joint diagnosis of
   business problems. Here task forces and project groups or *ad
   hoc* teams were created to integrate the organisation around
   the task.
2. Develop a shared vision of how to organise and manage for
   competitiveness.
3. Foster consensus for the new vision, competence to enact it,
   and cohesion to move it along. Strong leadership from the
   local manager is important at this point to overcome resistance to change.
4. Spread revitalisation to all departments (without pushing it
   from the top). The departments from which pioneers came
   have to rethink their roles and authority, to support their team
   members in the project. If each department has a chance to
   reinvent the wheel, to find its own way, real commitment will
   be greater.
5. Institutionalise the changes through formal policies, systems
   and structures – this comes near the end, not the beginning.
   Information systems? Better that they lag a little till everyone
   understands how the new approaches work. So, too, with
   personnel policies, quality procedures, customer service,
   control systems.
6. Monitor and adjust strategies in response to problems. Keep
   the task at the leading edge. In effect, you are creating a
   learning organisation that can adapt to change, and monitor
   its own behaviour – 'learning how to learn'.

The role of the centre in the successful cases was to make it easy
for tailor-made change to waft from one location to another,
maintaining momentum as well as high-profile local ownership.

Today's trends towards the centre specifying all processes is
likely to work against this more organic (and usually more

successful) model for change, because it disempowers everyone but the central teams or committees designing the processes.

The Japanese Manage

Ian Cunningham at Roffey Park, published in 1993 some research his college did with the Centre for Research into Organisation and Management at Sussex. They found that the Japanese do not have 'secrets' of management and leadership – they just do things a little more wholeheartedly and coherently.

Cunningham commented: 'The message is positive: UK managers who use effective planning, and who work to win support of their staff, can match the achievements of the best Japanese industrial supervisors.' Japanese leaders are able to link two important concepts:

- performance of subordinates;
- maintaining good relationships.

In Britain, these are too often viewed as opposites, and the resulting leadership subsides into either firm-but-fierce, or friendly-but-fluffy. When more managers and supervisors realise that their people *want* to meet deadlines and win, the UK may catch up.

Back in the Real World . . .

Meanwhile, the troops at the bottom of most large organisations are being told to expect all sorts of things that never actually happen:

- empowerment;
- communication;
- quality;
- excellence;
- change.

The troops are not the problem – the expectations are.

Empowerment is one of the biggest promises today. I worry because it will create the fiercest expectations – and the worst problems will probably be for the practical managers in the middle, as usual.

Notes

1. Henry Mintzberg (1973), *The Nature of Managerial Work*, Boston: MIT Sloane.

2. Michael Beer, R.A. Eisenstat and Bert Spector (1990), 'Why change programs don't produce change', *Harvard Business Review*, Boston; Nov.–Dec. 1990.

11

Don't Castrate Supervisors

Very few large organisations know how to empower their supervisors, yet these are the front-line managers on whose skill and enthusiasm the success of the organisation depends. Unless you spend the time to develop leaderless work groups, you can't empower people unless you first empower their supervisors.

Many organisations know, instinctively, how to disempower: I recall a large company in the car industry that decided to raise the calibre of its front-line management. After years of developing excellence from the shop floor, they 'improved management' by bringing in raw graduates as 'senior foremen' – over the heads of the best, most motivated foremen in the business. By the time management began to wonder about a drop in morale, the disenchanted foremen were muttering about 'young hotshots who don't know the business'; absenteeism and stress-related illness were rising, and not a single foreman expected ever again to win promotion. All their aspirations and opportunities had been capped, at a single stroke.

It doesn't take very many opportunities for advancement (half a dozen senior foremen in a large car factory?) to inspire a large population. Many people do not actively want promotion, but the idea that it is possible to try for it is still a motivator.

There is a more insidious, gradual form of castration – the

accumulation of fluff and felt in the middle of the organisation, which happens at the expense of the front-line manager. One by one, his tasks are monitored, then reported on, then statistics are sucked up to higher levels, until he has very little ability to decide anything. How many supervisors today have the right to decide on whether or not people are docked wages when they get to work late? The same cautiousness that erodes his room to manoeuvre also erodes his official information flow, so he is increasingly dependent on his grapevines.

A few organisations today are exploring this phenomenon, and bravely beginning to restore to the front-line manager some time-honoured tasks – like firing people. The next empowering step is to have the supervisor doing his own hiring. Beyond that, it might be possible to involve the entire team in the selection and development of its own members – the empowering possibilities are enormous!

Many an organisation no longer even calls the supervisor a manager any more, yet he manages the most expensive and demanding resource of all: its people.

The Organisational Eunuch

The organisational eunuch, in the absence of formally derived power, has to empower himself in other ways. This person, unable to build or create, retains the ability to sabotage other people's creations. In particular, the eunuch can and will destroy any programme to empower people.

Before you set out to empower supervisors, it might be wise to look around for the most cynical, argumentative, obstructive blockers in the system. Talk to a few of them individually, for an hour or more if possible. Look for hints of the things that demotivated them – and quietly look for any signals that might rekindle their enthusiasm. The blockers can do great harm but, properly managed, they can be early symbols of empowering.

It may depend on how long the organisational eunuch has been in this disempowered state. Does he or she retain a picture of an organisation where people had power to change things? People who spend their whole lives in disempowering organisations, like seventeenth-century castrati, have never known what it was to sing strong baritone lines.

There is an old American saying: 'Those who have, get.' Its corollary must be, 'Those who haven't, don't.' You cannot push empowerment into a place where no bedrock of trust exists.

You can empower people to move an organisation from zero to plus ten, but if you try to force empowerment into a minus-ten environment, like Cinderella's ugly stepsister trying on the glass slipper, you will merely end up with glass splinters in your feet – and worse mistrust than before.

That is not to say that within a typical department the local blocker cannot be treated to a slight enrichment of his diet. Remember why God loves sinners! Try a weekly meeting in his diary, with some strong rules about what his people are entitled to hear from him – backed up by rules about what he is entitled to hear from whom, when.

Communication is full of disempowering traps. Forceful top management says: 'We must speak direct to our people!' – and they send a letter to people's homes, or they make a video to show in the canteen. And one more task that once belonged to the front-line manager wafts away into the fluff.

There is another fluffy form of disempowering: *killing them with kindness*. The overloaded front-line manager who complains he has not been told is brought up sharply: 'You can't have read your minutes!' – 20 pages of close-typed text. Unless someone tells him the highlights, he might as well not get the minutes. People often overlook or disbelieve information until it becomes coherent. With organisation information, this usually means the second or third time that someone hears it, or when a trusted person explains it. Top management could take advantage of this phenomenon by sending front-line managers a one-page précis – but it seldom happens.

Empower, Then Develop

You have to empower your supervisors before you can start developing them. 'Supervisors' have many names: ward sister, team leader, branch manager, foreman, charge-hand. I shall use the term to mean any front-line manager who actually manages a team of people doing the work 'at the face'.

Empowering has to start at the front line, empowering front-line managers to manage. That means they need confidence as well as communication, the kind of confidence that comes with good, frequent, just-in-time training, a strong sense of purpose, and a belief that their work is valued.

Organisations get the supervisors (and the shop stewards) they deserve. A 1990 survey found that shop stewards in the UK are gradually disappearing – down from 54 per cent of work-places in 1984 to 38 per cent in 1990. Staff are more reluctant to take on the role, so elections for stewards go uncontested. Recognition of unions has also dropped, mainly due to plant closures rather than derecognition. In workplaces with more than 25 employees, recognition for collective bargaining was down from 66 per cent to 53 per cent.

With disempowered supervisors and disappearing stewards, many issues that should be solved locally are escalating to higher levels, clogging up the machinery that should be used to achieve better management. One more factor fuzzes up the focus on performance.

The two main elements that make up 'management style' are

- communication, and
- delegation.

When you increase these, the foremen can see and hear and feel the actions, never mind the exhortations.

People at the bottom of the organisation have a number of sources of information: the grapevine, the shop steward (if there is one), the TV and newspapers. But they need to depend on their sources, and the source they most want is the front-line manager, their own leader. Quite naturally, they want to be able to ask questions and receive dependable clarification on the spot.

The mellifluous 'reasons why' that often accompany higher-level decisions often need translating into the vernacular: 'He really means that TQM is going to be the next flavour of the month.' If that is true, people would rather hear it from a foreman than a shop steward. This particularly applies to negative decisions: 'They've turned down our project . . .' – people need to hear reasons why. Thus we get Nancy's Other Law of Leadership:

Never say 'No.' Say 'No, because . . .'

Communication has eroded badly in most large organisations. So has delegation. Only in delegating the real tasks to the front line can you begin to empower these key managers. And only when they feel they have some power can they begin to empower their people.

Fiddles and Freedoms

Some of the dirty work has to be delegated, too. Most supervisors these days find it fairly convenient to leave it to higher levels to cope with problems like petty theft. The union may try to protect the member who has been caught stealing, while a thousand other members find their freedoms further curtailed.

You have to face up to the fiddles. They breed cynicism. But there are fine lines; what about finishing early, or just doing your errands in company time? In a small organisation, it is quite natural to take time off for the dentist, and then work extra time when it is needed. In larger organisations, however, timekeeping takes on a more formal aspect – but it is only the front-line manager who knows what will be perceived by his people as 'fair'.

Many places have rules that make it easier to take the entire day off (with sick pay) when you need an hour to go to the dentist, than to take the hour and be docked for it. So the system not only turns a blind eye, it actually teaches people to be dishonest. Justice must be seen to be done. Too often, people see injustices done – and they remember, for a long time.

Thus people see their senior managers taking unnecessary business trips overseas with the holiday plane fare paid by the company, or driving when they could take a train, 'to get the mileage'. Where is the fine line between that and copying some papers for the PTA? Corporate ethics are debated near the top, but they are determined much nearer the bottom. Give this task back to the supervisor, along with clear-cut guidelines about what is expected of him and his people.

Love Your Supervisors

Most organisations are quite content to leave the front-line managers underqualified. They manage people, budgets, communications, with no training. They often have the responsibility but not the authority to manage these resources. Sometimes they feel like a 'buffer zone', only seen as managers when it suits higher management, otherwise kept as ill-informed as their troops.

Some organisations prefer to have their supervisors overqualified, but a manager needs to practise what he or she has been taught. There are people with HND or even DMS qualifications not being allowed to handle budgets!

Many able people have come 'up through the ranks', which is often a superb start for development. Many able people have also come from universities. It is the overnight switch from one model to another that can demotivate the front-line managers who still have aspirations.

Culture plays a part here. The civil service, for example, has clearly defined levels of management with structured training, but it seldom touches the front-line managers, who are called 'industrials' or 'technocrats' and thus assumed by the system not to need management skills. Similarly, nurses are promoted for their nursing skills; engineers are promoted for their engineering skills. This kind of promotion creates the 'string of beads' organisation chart, with one person on top of another, in a silly fiction of management that actually leaves things unmanaged. In the days of stability, these experts may not have needed as much training; they had a more direct say in choosing and training and deploying their own people. Today, they are simply disempowered people in under-managed systems, trying to change without the tools for the task.

The National Health Service in the UK differs in another way. The line manager is not usually the doctor. The highest paid people are at the coal face: urologists, surgeons, psychiatrists out there meeting and healing the 'customer'. The managers were until recently dismissed by the clinical experts as 'administrators'. The system is changing now, with managers coming in from outside, insisting on empowering employees, and the clinical people will be looking for budgets of their own to manage. The empowering may depend more on budget information than other forms of communication.

Some management experts these days proclaim that empowering is going to founder because supervisors and shop floor people do not have the capability to take on more responsibility. That is utter nonsense! It may take a little time for people who have been demotivated to respond to opportunities and begin to enjoy more involvement, but I have yet to meet a worker who has reached the limits of his or her abilities. The problem is invariably opportunity or attitude, not aptitude.

This is even more true for supervisors, who were certainly able enough to be promoted over their fellow workers in the first place. Many have become turned-off; very few are not capable enough for the task. Almost anyone can be turned on again if you find out (ask!) what stops them doing better work, and then help them to eliminate the barriers.

In most organisations, two steps are necessary before supervisors can be expected to grow:

- accept that they are part of management, and
- demonstrate that recognition credibly.

When John Egan was at Jaguar, he used to attend personally or send a member of his top team whenever a first-line manager won an award.

One senior BT manager, Joan Sweeney, attended front-line briefings for all her 1167 engineering staff at least once a year, and held regular workshops for groups of her front-line managers. Since her death, BT's empowered front-line managers are a lasting memorial; Joan Sweeney's people still stand out in BT surveys for their outstanding scores in management and morale.

One way of looking at today's organisation needs is to focus on *development*. In addition to organisation development and management development, a few leading lights are beginning to consider *employee* development. Figure 11.1 shows one way in which they might fit together.

Figure 11.1 Employee Development Model

12

Empowering through the Networks

The companies that succeed in changing (and empowering their people) consciously or unconsciously use networks to help achieve their changes. This chapter explains how to build and maintain networks, either within a single organisation or across a number of them. It also explores ways to build and use external networks to support changes inside.

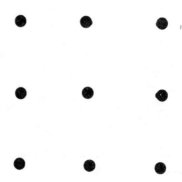

Figure 12.1 The Nine-dot Puzzle

Outside energy is often necessary to solve internal problems. Remember the old nine-dot puzzle? This demands that you connect all the dots with only four straight lines, without lifting the pencil from the paper.

Figure 12.2 illustrates the solution. I often show this to consultants when they become conceited about clients wanting their wisdom. It is not usually their wisdom that is needed, but their 'outside-ness'. People inside know what is necessary; their organisation has simply not listened to them.

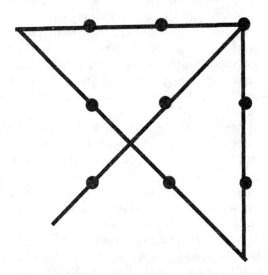

Figure 12.2 The Solution

There is plenty of research to show that companies prosper in direct proportion to the richness and flow of informal information inside: the grapevine, the jungle telegraph, the rumour mill. People believe what they hear from trusted colleagues – more than they believe the house journal, or the team briefing, or the notice-board. One way to enrich the internal flow is simply to encourage the informal networks that are already lurking around the edges, in the canteens, at the sports club.

An informal network may be a few people who lunch together sometimes, or hundreds who receive the same newsletter or go to the same annual conference. Some professional societies claim to be networks, but I see them as hierarchies – the real networks within them are likely to revolve around local branches.

Windows in Organisation Walls

Informal networks create windows in organisation walls without damaging the sense of membership of the people inside those walls – that is one reason we need them so desperately in large organisations, where people have to build new links rapidly and develop flexibility from quite rigid historical structures. Frightened people (and too many *are* frightened in today's organisations) dare not risk themselves in new structures, but many will take comfort (and new values) from voluntary participation in border-crossing events. Other people's successful experience can be empowering.

The informal network depends on trust. In a formal organisation, like a marriage, loyalty is necessary. But in a network, like a friendship, you can have many links without endangering the others.

I 'belong' to the Real Time Club, Devonshire House Management Club, the Railway Study Association, the Edinburgh Employee Comms breakfast group, Women in Management, the board of the nation's smallest radio station, the development committee of the Scottish Museums Council, a guild of spinners and dyers, a number of local good works, the Killiecrankie Social Club, several informal lunching groups of professionals, the executive messes of several client companies, a swimming group for antiquarian large ladies, and a few other networks.

Someone else brings to one of these tables information from an investment club, a great books group, a ski club, a PTA, and so on. Among the skiers is a good man impatient with his present job, and among the personnel people is a director from a good company where the skier would fit better. Click! They find each other. The networks work because people in several of them trust each other.

Starting a network is easy. You are interested in something, and you phone a few people you know who might know something about it, suggest a time and place to meet, and ask who else might be interested. The cost (minimum) is a little time and some cups of tea. Networks *can* be built on written or electronic contact, but the trust and information levels are inevitably higher when they are based on personal contact.

Uncertainty is increasing in large organisations. When you don't know what you're going to have to know about tomorrow, it is impossible to store up all the information you might need about everything. So you operate by building a map of who knows about what – or who-knows who-knows. You map nodes into different networks, and as long as the trust is undiminished, you can receive and send information quite liberally. (I once sold an MGB by telling everyone I met for three weeks that it was available. The phone call, when it came, was from a friend of one of my accountant's other clients.)

Networks are less expensive than consultants, and sometimes a more credible way of bringing outside-ness to an organisation. They have to be built and maintained, and they cost a little time and energy, but the results can be splendid:

- new ideas;
- current gossip;
- leads to fill information needs;
- reinforce formal information;
- exchange of experience;
- avoiding others' pitfalls;
- support for innovators;
- 'licensing' of shared interests;
- a general increase in confidence.

Few networkers have the energy, money or time to attend to all the meetings, gatherings, lunches and phone calls that make up network membership. But even the most remote, abstract specialist may gain from access to a link into a colleague's network. The 'contact man' in the Belbin team role scoring is the link for the team into the networks.

In *The Yin and Yang of Organizations* (1980)[1] I spelt out the 'rules' for building and maintaining networks. So many people have handed round scruffy Xerox copies that it is time to publish a new version, only slightly changed from the original. A dozen more years using and enjoying networks have not changed my perceptions appreciably.

You cannot set up a system to increase the quality and quantity of informal information in an organisation, but you can encourage the networks. You cannot plan a grapevine, but you can fertilise it. It is no coincidence that the companies that survive and thrive on their informal links seldom cut down on phoning or faxing, no matter how strict their targets. And business travel, too, can feed a network.

Networks for Informal Information

The networks that create this informal information flow are somewhat different from the networks that support direct action. Once you distinguish between the two, you can do whatever is necessary to support the kinds of networks you need. Once you see that a network exists to bring more information to its members, then you want:

- open, easy access;
- many members with different experiences, outlooks, sources;
- some unprogrammed time for people to chat about the things that interest them.

Thus we have Foy's Law of Networking:

The effectiveness of a network is inversely proportional to its formality

The more chance members have to chat informally, the better they know one another, the more informal information they inject into the network. One of the more interesting properties of information is that you don't lose it by giving it away.

Every residential course is a *de facto* network, at least for a while. Some organisations have regular reunions or refreshers so that members can maintain their sense of membership. Most experienced participants on management courses know that more than half the value comes not from the formal teaching and classroom work, but from the meals, coffee breaks, and sessions around the bar. If the information is no more elaborate than rugby scores and 'I'm OK, you're OK,' it is still valuable for building confidence and trust.

Membership in a network is almost completely in the hands of the individual. You are a member as long as a few of the other people still recognise you. Your degree of membership depends on how often you meet other members, and how much information you bring and take away. People who naturally belong to a number of networks can be very valuable for carrying information between them, though they seldom focus sufficiently to tend a single network. Both are useful.

A certain threshold of information flow is necessary to build a network, as RCA learned when they tried to build the pioneering colour TV network. Until they could attract enough people to buy colour sets, there wasn't enough money to make good colour programmes, but without good colour programmes, people don't buy colour sets.

In most business environments, you can surmount the threshold rapidly by bringing together several good speakers who disagree about the topic, and inviting as many people who know something about it as possible. Then give them plenty of time to argue with each other and the speakers. If they have a good time and a new insight or two, they will probably welcome the idea of regular gatherings.

The network convener cannot plan the new insights, because they are different for each participant, according to his or her own interests and experience.

A network needs a focus, not a goal

The topic gives your potential network its focus. As soon as you inject into an information network a specific goal, beyond 'keeping up to date about X', or 'keeping in touch with each other', you are driving away those members or potential members who have different (or opposite) goals. Their inputs might be the most useful informal information for the members who do share the goal.

Keep the goals for action networks. To retain a network's integrity for information flow, let members use it to create their own subgroups for specific goals, but keep the network itself goal-free. I have seen several good information networks lose valuable members when they decided to lobby for a particular piece of legislation. They might have kept all the members, and improved the laws, just by inviting various lawmakers along to normal gatherings, where members with varying views could do their own lobbying, thus giving the lawmakers more information and avoiding the trap of trying to create one uniform (and probably useless) formal view.

A network needs a spider at the centre of the web

Chairmen are not a necessity of life for networks; they rarely do more than preserve the components. Chairmen seldom contribute as much to the networks they support as the humble person (it is usually only one) who maintains the list of members' names and addresses and phone numbers. The web-building spider (secretary?) works not from a position of power but more as a servant of the members. Dependable access is one of the spider's most endearing characteristics. Another must be some sense that the work itself is worthwhile; few networks appreciate their spiders as much as they extol the virtues of their seemingly more important chairmen.

A network needs a phone number, not a headquarters building

Parkinson's Law pointed out the deadly effects of the Edifice Complex. As soon as people at the centre of a network begin to worry about paying the rent, or repairing the fabric of the new HQ, their ability to answer questions about individual members' interests diminishes. The spider's phone number is the key. In smaller networks, the spider's role can even rotate, as long as all members know where to phone for information.

A network needs a phone and address list more than it needs a journal

A very small group may be able to convene itself by phone, but beyond half a dozen it helps to have a more formal mechanism. My 30-strong employee communications group in Edinburgh meets every other month on the last Friday at 8 am for bacon butties and a professional update. People arrive early so they have time to chat to each other before we have a professional update session. In a typical period I will receive at least four or five phone calls from members with questions or answers to shared concerns.

I have recently been dis-joining old networks like the multi-thousand BIM (now IM) that stopped supporting local branches so well, and depended more on heavy-handed headquarters publications.

One of the least helpful publications for networks are bylaws. The lists of members get to the heart of things. I found out about one network because the head of a small network had a card on his notice-board with the names and phone numbers of 30 other presidents of local firms. 'We do more business among ourselves since we started this club,' he said. 'It cuts down on transportation costs, and I think I'm getting better deliveries because the guy you meet over lunch doesn't want to let you down.' The purpose of the club was to talk about the problems of managing small firms in its region. Getting new business was simply one of those problems.

A network needs first names

Lists of members tend to be rather formal, more so in Britain than the United States. I seldom refer to the list from one group with more than 200 members – it gives every detail about each of their institutions but no first names! So the thick book lives in a bookcase in another room. At the other end of the spectrum, the short list with only first initials and company names is also less than helpful. Like many others, I file by first name and face. I cannot quite remember Gerald's last name or which of several companies he was with. Three possibilities have the letter 'G'. Oh, well, I have other things to do besides call the wrong person.

While on the subject of names, it is useful for groups that do not get together often to have name badges, which should carry full names, in large, readable type. I never bother reading typed badges, especially when very legible, professional-looking badges are so easy to produce nowadays.

A network needs groups rather than committees

Networks operate most effectively if they have gatherings rather than meetings. I have nothing against committees and meetings, but they reinforce the formal side, and have a dreadful tendency to focus on objectives and performance, even when these are not quite appropriate. They are hamstrung by chairman and agendas, constraining the information to that which is formal and related to the specified goal. *Throw them out!* My husband, a superb chairman who suspects me of generally anti-agenda tendencies, puts it another way: 'Keep them where they belong – to support authority where authority is needed, not to decide who shall share information and who shall not.'

A group meets because its members share some interest, and information flows because they have time to talk informally to one another.

A network needs an annual bash

Most of these are called conventions or conferences or reunions or seminars. From the networking viewpoint, people in large organisations usually need at least a critical mass of the faithful, gathered for at least 24 hours – an opportunity for the shared hangover, or the feast, or the annual poker game, or any other generally accepted symbol of their occasional but continuing togetherness. They need enough formal input to satisfy the members (and their accountants) that honour (and business) has been done. If a network has no such ceremonial gathering, its links are likely to rust, and livelier subgroups or supergroups that do convene regularly will supplant it.

Self-destruction is not necessarily a bad thing. Some networks should self-destruct, as 'temporary systems', when they have fulfilled their members' needs for information.

An information network can have quite a strong focus, without expecting any action from the members. I remember an in-company Women's Careers Discussion Group, a healthy fort-nightly gathering of secretaries and professional people, who invited a woman from another organisation to talk about her career for each meeting. The result of the meeting was a little more confidence for most of its members, better connection, and a much healthier flow of company information around the corridors of power.

Hierarchies need order. Networks need minimum bureau-cracy. The two need not conflict, as long as the flatness and voluntary nature of the network are respected, and people allocate time to be unallocated.

Most effective networks in business have to operate within constraints. We are somehow unable to tell ourselves the whole truth, that we're going to a gathering because it's fun, so we work hard to make it useful as well (sometimes at the expense of the fun). Our consciences demand that we work very hard to compensate for enjoying a set of new faces or favourite faces. On the other hand, if we lean over too far on the side of orderliness and control and achievement, we may lose the zest that brings the members of a network we most wanted to see.

Networks for Action

A group with a shared objective and a need to take action still has a need for informal information to flow. But it also needs enough structure to make sure that focussed action happens. This means review, monitoring, people telling each other what they have done since last time – in other words, management. Yet for maximum motivation, members of an action network must continue to own themselves and their activities.

Many effective lobbying groups fit into this category: people from different places gather together (often voluntarily) to pursue a shared goal.

An action network or task force might be useful inside an organisation to cope with a problem that crossed many boundaries. ScotRail has a 'focus group' to monitor employee communications, with members from a number of different parts of the company. Dundee's hospitals have a similar, smaller monitoring group for employee communications, with people from Training and Personnel as well as Quality and Resource Management.

Some excellent boards of directors have discovered that the needs for informal information and formal, goal-related action can both be met.

One board meets once a month for half a day as a board, concentrating on relatively short-term action and formal review of prepared papers. Then a fortnight later virtually the same members meet for a full day as the Quality Council, taking a longer view, discussing issues much less formally, taking time over lunch to chat to each other and move about. Several times a year they go away to a hotel to look at even longer-term issues; one or two younger managers are often invited to join them for a meal during these special meetings.

Groups for effective action need this kind of balance between informal, trust-building, information time, and focused, goal-oriented action time. The two go together like Yin and Yang.

Note

1. Nancy Foy (1980), The Yin and Yang of Organizations, London: Grant McIntyre; New York: Morrow.

13

Empowering Starts with Listening

People in organisations have a great deal to say. Some of it could be of great value to the organisation – these are the people most expert in getting their jobs done. Sometimes, however, one is reminded of the old Buddhist question: If a tree falls in the forest, and there is no one listening, does it make a sound?

Every manager has ways of listening to his or her people. Most feel they do listen, but not so many are seen to listen. A little more effort here could return considerable benefit for the organisation. The manager can not only listen to people, but also help them feel that their management wants to hear.

The organisation itself usually has a number of listening processes, which indicate that at the most senior levels listening is valued; for example:

- elected representatives;
- word of foot (management by walking around);
- meeting feedback (see Chapter 14);
- suggestion scheme;
- anonymous speak-up programme;
- 'open door';

- letters to the editor of the house magazine;
- surveys (see Chapter 17).

Most of these channels are described in 'An A–Z of Communication' (see pages 227–46). The more listening posts there are, the stronger the structure, but (like the management's credibility) *it still rests on the individual employee believing that his own manager wants to hear what he has to say.*

Formal Channels for Listening

Management have let themselves misunderstand formal consultation, thinking it is the unions who should be listening and the managers talking. When this happens, performance skills are used to hide the absence of listening skills.

Typically, at the beginning of a joint council meeting, the senior manager gives a talk about the state of the business. Seldom does he ask the senior representative to tell him how the business feels from his viewpoint, nor does the rep volunteer this useful information.

The topics for joint consultation have gradually been constrained to hygiene factors, so much so that any chance for constructive listening about how the business runs at the workplace level is lost. It has become taboo to talk about the one subject where reps have real information to contribute: what is happening down there.

Behind the scenes, it is the unions who determine the agendas. They fill them with what they want to learn from management. Members of the management team then work like Trojans to gain and keep control of the meeting. Sensible union officials sit back and listen, for they are in full control of the information flow, and they have silently reversed the process: it is not the management consulting the workforce, but the workforce consulting the management, as it sees fit.

Colin Minton's analysis of a year's agenda items in one large company showed 196 from the unions, and four from management. Many of the items were of mutual interest, but management did 95 per cent of the talking. Some consultation!

So management often wastes its listening opportunities through this channel, while unions have developed it so that they gain much information and give away very little. Managers say:'The unions are only interested in negotiating. We are interested in constraining their ambitions. We will tell them what they need to know. We are certainly not going to listen to them!' The unions smile serenely and retain control.

How do you change this situation? Very simple: ask questions, and listen to the answers. Ask some more: 'What do your members feel about . . .?' All those questions you are paying to have investigated by surveys can be interesting for both parties in a joint consultative meeting. It seems a shame to waste the opportunity.

Information is *not* like money. When you spend money it is gone. When you give away information, you still have it, and the person you gave it to should give you some of his in return. So at the end of the transaction there should be twice as much information in circulation, and each of you knows what the other knows. It is the only game where two plus two equals five.

Walking the Job

Fritz Schumacher of *Small is Beautiful* fame often said:

> If you want to grow good crops, the best fertiliser is the farmer's boot. You don't grow good things by sitting in your office. You need to feel the soil, see how things are growing, listen, check that what you think is happening is actually happening.

My neighbour John Forbes has always been this kind of farmer. When horses gave way to tractors, he insisted on driving everywhere on his farm at the speed of the old horses. 'Otherwise you miss things,' he explained.

You also miss things if you go too fast in listening. Managers who are hung up on status don't want to be asked questions they can't answer immediately; they can't admit they don't know something. It is somewhat revolutionary for a senior manager to admit the truth: that the person who knows most about a job is the one who does it.

One thing a manager can do when he walks the job is look at what people are putting in the scrap bins. This is better than a dozen reports. If there are surprising items or quantities, a neutral question can reveal problems long before they show up on paper.

Walking the job is too often treated as a royal procession, set up by the PR man. One car factory (at least) had its 'golden mile' for visiting executives, resplendent with fresh yellow lines. The operators nearest the route had clean uniforms, but the rest of the place looked like a rubbish tip. The executives all knew it was going on, but none chose to leave the well-trodden ritual path.

In another factory, the local manager bragged that he was in close touch with the floor. In fact, he valued information 'from the boys' above that which his direct subordinates told him. He was right: because he was a hair-trigger manager who exploded with rage whenever bad news arrived, none of his subordinates liked telling him anything. His meetings grew shorter and blander. The manager was actually quite sound, albeit hot-tempered, so be began to sense that people were keeping things from him. That is when he began touring the floor looking for trouble. A few people enjoyed the process, but most employees judiciously disappeared when he arrived, because no one likes tattling and getting people in trouble. So the manager's sources diminished still further. Along the way he forgot about the importance of good news in the management mix.

One of my favourite managers is a good walker. One subordinate commented:

> He goes up and asks people about their jobs. He's interested, and he listens. The next time he sees them he tends to ask something more, and they tell more easily. Pretty soon he understands what's going on – sometimes better than the managers in between.

The language of management tends not to help the listening process. People on the shop-floor talk in plain and sometimes vivid vernacular. Management information is usually written in third-party passive, with everything qualified, iffed and butted. It's jargon-ridden, obscure, and foggy verbiage. (The FOG index counts the number of words per sentence, plus the proportion of words with three or more syllables. You can get a FOG count on some computer grammar-checks now.)

For too many managers the motto is still: 'Don't keep it simple! They might understand what you meant to tell them.'

The Suggestion Scheme

In most organisations the suggestion scheme actually suppresses people's natural inventiveness. Formal schemes tend to suffer three main problems:

- They get too soon old and too late wise!
- They take too long.
- They generate too little trust.

The typical scheme was launched decades ago and never brought up to date – witness the £100 million company that thought £20 was a proper award for a practical suggestion that saved the company half a million.

Innovation is an exciting, 'now' kind of thing, yet most suggestion schemes take for ever to process a suggestion ('Papers come back with the dusty smell of lingering death,' says consultant Colin Minton). It can take two years for a response to your original form to arrive, and then they say it will take five years to measure the value. You might receive an award before you retire. Why bother?

The typical suggestion scheme breeds mistrust. We're dealing with money here, and concepts of fairness are never far from the surface. Ambiguity banishes trust. If people do not know who is entitled to suggest what, they suspect the worst: 'Do you have to be a best friend of the Engineering Manager to get a maximum award?'

One large manufacturer has its scheme administered by an accountant with the sharpest pencil in the country. He prides himself on saving the company money by finding reasons to reject suggestions. No one ever showed him the value of involvement, of recognition, of empowering people.

Listening on the Grapevine

My 'networking', your 'grapevine', his 'scurrilous scuttlebut', the politician's 'mole'. The grapevine is a contentious element of employee communications.

The academics give us clear evidence that the single factor which correlates most closely with corporate profit is not investment, nor research, nor marketing; it is the richness of informal information through the organisation. In other words, over the long term the better the grapevines, the higher the profit.

A few companies that recognise this go to great lengths to encourage the internal networks: reunions of old courses, company dinners, coffee breaks, functional conferences, rest areas. Wherever people get together they are exchanging important information about their work.

People prefer to get the real story from authentic sources. In the absence of the real story, people make up their own stories to fit the data they have. When the parables are nasty, they reflect a nasty underlying view of the organisation (which is useful information in itself). When people don't believe the information they are given formally, they have to depend more on the grapevine, and they resent it. The information they receive is more hostile, and they feel less associated with the organisation.

The grapevine is not accountable. Every other source can be traced to people who can be held accountable. The grapevine is just 'there'. It may be believed, but it has no authority.

Grapevine information can be harmful: the gossip, the morale-sappers, stories that denigrate management, stories that encourage people to think that their own jobs or tasks are at risk. Such rumours fill a void of management's own making.

The organisation can help informal information flow, but can never control the grapevines. The trick is to make sure the formal information keeps within reasonable reach of the informal grapevines – which means managers, too, need to listen on the grapevines.

Listening can be Learned

As musicians know, some people have ears that are more finely tuned than others. So it is with listening to what people really want to say; some listeners are certainly better than others. But even the worst listener can gain more information by learning a few simple rules, and practising ways which show that he is listening (in general 'she' tends to be a better listener than 'he' does).

Engineers know it takes two elements to set up communication: a sender and a receiver. There are problems if the sender does not send clearly or loudly enough. There are worse problems when the receiver does not receive what is sent.

When the person who is trying to communicate does not have the other person's attention, no matter how benign the receiver, it is natural to feel that the receiver is really saying:

- You're unimportant.
- I don't trust you.
- I don't want to get involved in this.
- Your feelings are invalid.
- Your thinking is wrong.

The natural reaction, in turn, is defensive. The sender's resistance rises. Even the seemingly 'helpful' leaping to conclusions (we all do it!) is rejected, or accepted without taking any responsibility. The sender stops communicating, and subsides into what he or she thinks the non-listening receiver wants to hear. Mistrust increases both ways, and the relationship is harmed. The sender's self-confidence drops, and potential problems escalate.

When you view listening as a skill that can be learned, you start with the key question: what does the sender want? And underneath this: what does the sender feel about this? That is useful information. There are also things you can do to get the process moving:

- *Silence* Good silence, good eye contact, even the old trick of putting your head a little on one side, can be encouraging.

- *Show attention* No fiddling with your hands, or shuffling papers. Just a relaxed, alert body language.
- *Nod acknowledgement* This can be a very positive non-verbal signal.
- *Repeat key phrases* Do not repeat parrot-fashion, but thoughtful repetition in a 'Did I get that right?' tone of voice.
- *Paraphrase* When the sender slows, or grows tentative, you can check your understanding and reinforce how well you are listening by saying: 'You mean . . .?'

As a receiver you need to show interest and acceptance of what the sender wants you to know. There are more positive things you can do as the communication continues and you are both certain you understand the situation:
- look at alternative approaches;
- explore consequences;
- reveal your own feelings;
- share your experiences.

If the topic is a task, you can suggest resources, look at soft spots in the discussion, and help strengthen them so the sender can gain support from others. If the topic is behaviour (the sender's, the receiver's, or someone else's) this can be an opportunity to discuss how you communicate with each other, and to make commitments to new behaviour, and to plan ways to monitor it.

Timing and sincerity are both important. You can speak too soon and cause the sender to go into his shell, or too late and give the impression that you didn't really listen. You can be too analytical, or use the same phrase so often that it becomes counterproductive.

Sometimes you need to confront the sender, not just listen encouragingly (even senders can be wrong). If you respond without empathy, in a non-caring tone of voice, the 'listening' words will sound cynical. Worst of all is to use listening 'techniques' in order to draw out a person, and then revert to inattentiveness, making the relationship even worse because of the built-up expectations.

If listening is done in an active, empathetic way, the sender has a better chance to define his own problem, and take responsibility for the solution. There is less temptation for either party to blame others, and more chance for insight and a more open, honest relationship.

Good listening can be an asset to managers walking about 'to catch people doing things right'. Its value can be reinforced by surveys when employees appraise managers' performance in part by how well they listen.

14

Team Meetings without Bumf

Whenever I go into a new organisation I try to jot down the way people refer to their meetings. In hospitals, for example, they tend to be called 'staff meetings', while BT people call them 'group meetings'. Whatever they are called, they are about talking to people at work, and listening to their comments and questions in return.

Team Briefing and Cascade Concerns

Very seldom do people use the term 'team briefing' to refer to a useful meeting. More often than not, the term has been devalued by people's experience – it comes to mean long, boring meetings, where the leader reads out verbatim a number of items that aren't very relevant.

Classic team briefing was an excellent discipline, derived from the military model, in which a firm system was put in place, supervisors were trained, and someone monitored that briefings actually happened. Top management commitment was evident in that it was an expensive system to operate. So far so good; it was right to insist that every employee was entitled to be informed.

But here we meet a basic, structural fallacy. Front-line managers in large organisations tend not to be as highly trained as their military counterparts, and their organisational information tends to be fuzzier, less immediate. In large organisations team briefing almost always became a one-way cascade, from the top down. The only discussion built into the discipline was enough to make sure that people understood what they had been told. What was originally intended, the supervisor telling his people what he wanted and reasons why, became a charade, with the disempowered, often disinformed supervisor telling his people what someone else wanted (usually without reasons why). A cascade, by its very nature, is made up of information that interests the top. Worse still, the machinery tended to emphasize a core brief, which usually went down verbatim from the chief.

The larger the organisation, the surer and sooner the untended team briefing system silts up with top-down nonsense. In one large technical company I once had to kill a core brief that had grown to eight pages of closely printed, over-designed parchment!

No one in any normal organisation (where a modicum of blame might float around) is willing to cut one precious word of his boss's prose. *No matter how many exhortations there are in the training to peel off grandpa's bumf and add items of local interest, no one ever does.* Team briefing becomes another form of lip-service, with only the most daring and independent managers willing to drop the bumf and talk about things their people care about. The core brief, repeated parrot-fashion down all the cascades, is a credibility-killer. Every manager who doesn't own it but has to tell it verbatim is losing some of his own power in the eyes of his own people. He knows it and his self-confidence diminishes; they know it and his credibility diminishes.

Many large organisations recognise that formal employee communication needs to be renewed after a certain period. During 1991–2 Regional Railways brought in the Industrial Society to launch a completely new team briefing system. This caused particular concern among one large group of engineers, who were still dutifully attending regular team briefing meetings from the system installed seven years earlier. Their system was completely silted up, boring, un-brief, no time for teams, but the overloaded engineers stolidly maintained it, even so. When the new system came in they were alarmed and distressed, because they thought they would have to have *two* boring briefs in place of one. Because of the size of the organisation (and the unquestioning obedience of engineers) it took months before the company realised the situation and clarified the requirements.

Team Briefing Repair?

In most places, it is much easier to start from scratch, to install a robust, new two-way face-to-face communication mechanism down at the coalface, than to repair the flawed team briefing.

You do not have to throw out all the bath-water with the old baby. Check the credibility of the name in different departments. Keep the schedule (if it still works), and whatever workable ways you might have had to monitor that meetings were happening. If there is a workable one-page summary sheet, keep on using it. The most important place to start fresh is the content.

Me First

Get top management out of the act. Supervisors know what their people are concerned about. To turn team briefing on its head, first convene the supervisors in a single department or division (less than 50 supervisors, thus probably less than 500 people). Let them work out for themselves what information their people want, and how often they want it. A helpful person from Personnel will probably need to be involved, because Personnel owns much of the information people care about: policies or changes that affect overtime, lunch hours, image clothing, fire drills, other 'me' things.

This might be the time to institute a Nissan-type five minutes a day meeting – but only if you have Nissan-type supervisors who are good at developing their people (and managing time).

Performance

Forget the organisation performance for a while. Each group deserves a chance to look at its own performance, the 'us' focus. Only when that is well established will people be interested in the 'them' figures. The supervisor can review proposed topics with his boss, obtaining answers wherever possible to questions he knows his people will ask. An adept supervisor might come back with department or division figures and explain them in terms of a team's own performance.

Feed the Foremen

Reconvene the supervisors regularly to discuss issues about the division's or unit's performance, and to give them advance information (and reasons why) that they can pass on to their people. For too long, in too many organisations, they have been

Figure 14.1 Meeting Notes

left out of management communication: 'I usually hear about everything from my troops,' they say.

Meeting Notes

It can be helpful to have a member of the team take brief notes. I use a one-page sheet like Figure 14.1, with a border around the outside, to suggest to the scribe that the notes should not be more than the one page. This meeting note can then be copied, filed, and posted on whatever notice-board the rest of the team uses.

Very seldom does every single member of a team attend every single meeting. Nor do they have to. Those who are busy elsewhere, or off sick, or on holiday, etc do deserve respect in the form of an accessible record of what people discussed at the meeting, and any decisions or actions that resulted.

This, in my terms, is 'machinery', workable, available, simple. If you head the meeting notes with the team's name, it will also support the sense of membership.

Just the Facts, Ma'am

If supervisors are allowed to concentrate on giving their people the facts that affect them, and the reasons, then the natural outcome will be better understanding – and people who understand are on the way to being empowered. But too frequently missing from all this has been the facts, and the reasons why, from the bottom up. If plans from the top down are perceived as unworkable, how should that information be sent back up? Meeting notes can do the trick (absolving the supervisor of blame). Stores problems, holiday schedules, all sorts of factors can conspire to make the top-down 'tough but achievable target' into the bottom-up, unreachable demotivator.

The Pocket Card

When formal meetings are only once a month it is difficult to develop relevant, timely information. For weekly or daily meetings, supervisors often carry around a card in their pocket, on which to note questions from team members, or topics for discussion.

Rules of Thumb

Some simple rules for communication meetings may be useful. These originated with the Industrial Society for team briefing, and are amended by my own experience revitalising silted-up briefing systems in large organisations.

1. Team meetings should be *face-to-face, in teams*. You need discussion, and this reinforces team spirit, and the knowledge that everyone else knows about that item.
2. They should normally be *led by the team leader*. Sometimes a group member can substitute as competence and confidence grow.
3. They should be as *regular as clockwork*. Deferring a meeting tells people what management really thinks about them.
4. They should be *brief*. Five minutes a day is better than two hours a month.
5. Content should be *relevant – me* and *us*, not *them*. Any 'them' that has to be discussed should be in terms of what it means for 'us'.
6. They should be *monitored*. Meetings are central to the way information moves in an organisation. The supervisor's boss should sit in at least twice a year, and more senior managers should ask about meeting content as they walk about.

The classic Industrial Society 'four P' agenda for a useful meeting is:

1. *Performance* Review the team's progress and performance against its targets. If a target will be missed, what remedies are available? How can quality be improved, or costs cut? How does the team know it is winning?
2. *Policy* Are there any changes that affect the team? Explain what, why, and what the implications are for the team.
3. *People* New faces, moves, retirements within the team, thanks for jobs well done, accommodation concerns, any outside appointments that might interest the team.
4. *Points for action* Review the meeting – 'Anything else for next time?' – record feedback, note questions that have to be referred elsewhere for answers.

Certain questions can help a supervisor prioritise the information at hand; 'What does this mean to my team?' or 'What do we need to do about it?' If the answers are 'Not a lot,' or 'Nothing', the item can go at the end of the priority list. This type of agenda usually takes about half an hour in a typical team. Some groups add another half-hour for discussion; others like to have members give progress reports about their projects, or invite someone from another group to discuss joint interests. The important thing is to make sure the meeting belongs to the supervisor and the team, not the chairman and his cascade.

Many organisations have special meeting rooms, but I am convinced the gathering in the workplace, or around the supervisor's desk, works just as well. It does not even matter if people have to stand up, as the meeting should not take long enough to get uncomfortable.

Yes, supervisors need training to run meetings well, but, even more important, they need good information! Once that is assured, and they have held a few meetings, most supervisors will know what they want to learn – how to generate feedback from the floor, using flipcharts, how to get started. Coaching by the communications manager is often the best form of training at first. Then, once they are meeting regularly, small groups of supervisors can meet for a day or so using video to record and learn from their own performances.

There are various ways in which meetings can be audited or monitored. The boss regularly sitting in is one of the best, especially if he or she feeds back perceptions to the supervisor. It is even better if the boss also holds regular meetings, using best practice and setting an example.

I have seen an elaborate audit form which checks on how the leader prepared, the use of visual aids, timekeeping, how the group's performance was discussed or analysed, whether the ideas of members were solicited or acted upon, whether previous questions and issues received feedback, and how involved the team members seemed. This may be quite useful after all supervisors have had training and experience, it is somewhat formidable for the early stages of development.

The fastest way for good team meetings to develop into a culture is to make sure people see good meeting leadership being recognised and rewarded. If employees themselves get a chance to score their leaders on the usefulness of their meetings, and higher management takes their perceptions into account in appraising team leaders, then improvement will be rapid, as BT, IBM and others have shown.

Upward Communication Channels

The best employee communications includes strong channels for information to flow upwards, so that management can perceive internal pressures and opportunities for change. Management walkabout or sitabout and suggestion schemes were discussed in chapter 13 on listening and surveys are explored in Chapter 17.

Charles Hobley, BT's personnel and quality director for world-wide networks, wrote to all his managers, to encourage them to work together and thus make the feedback loop from team meetings work effectively. He said:

> We believe it will help us all to do our jobs better and to give our customers a better service. After all, a team that feels its views are respected and that gets its questions answered is likely to be more effective.

Feedback from Teams

Formal meeting feedback forms are seldom sufficient to keep higher management aware of real issues, though a few firms use forms rigorously, and gain an auditable process in quality terms (the form shown in Figure 14.1 is for the use of team members themselves, not the higher-ups). Looking at it from the other direction, though, I do like the systems that monitor questions which require answers from higher levels.

Supervisor Meetings

Some of the best feedback comes from regular management discussions with groups of supervisors, who often raise and clarify matters about which their people are concerned. Such face-to-face gatherings also give the supervisors a chance to explore more reasons why, and their managers a chance to monitor communications regularly. Ideally, a manager meets regularly with his supervisors, and they bring their hand-written meeting topics along, so they can add or expand items, and pick up things others propose to cover – a polite process which allows the manager to make sure that supervisors are doing their meeting planning in advance, without being heavy-handed about monitoring them.

15

Performance Measures

Empowering starts with good, factual feedback. Everyone who invests his working hours in an organisation wants to know, and deserves to know, at least two things: 'What am I supposed to be doing?', and 'How am I doing?' It is astounding how few people receive regular answers to these two questions.

As we noted in Chapter 2, unless people have better ways of winning', they measure the quality and quantity of tea breaks, or the number of pens they can take home, or even the number of customers they can frustrate, simply to reassure themselves that they really exist in the organisation.

The organisation wins by giving people something more worthwhile to measure – their own performance. It meets their own needs, their management's needs, and the organisation's needs. It creates win–win games, but it is anything but easy.

Is Money the Right Measure?

Performance has to be measured in the units that make sense to that person or group. A production person might make 75 carburettor valve assemblies in a day; his team might put together

400 carburettors in a week, and the plant might make 1000 vehicles in a month. That operator cares less about the vehicles than he does about his valves. The managing director, on the other hand, cares more about the vehicles and the money they represent than he does about the valves – until a hold-up in supplies to the person making the valves actually delays output of entire vehicles.

It ought to be the managing director's job to make sure that the operator appreciates the part his valves play in the vehicle as a whole, and to give him reasons to be proud of the vehicle. It is usually the foreman or supervisor who has to translate the language of managing directors into terms that refer to carburettor valves.

This is one reason why money is not a very good 'me' measure, outside finance and billing departments. The enormous effort in some organisations to teach people all about company accounts is an uphill battle. People at workplace level seldom have responsibility for the money they have to spend. It is doled out to them in penny pieces. They might feel quite proprietary about a proposed investment; 'our four million for new machines' can be taken away from them, but too seldom do they have the actual spending of it.

That is one reason why spending exercises can be very empowering. Money makes sense when it is yours to spend, and spending together is almost as good a form of communion as eating together. Even a team trip to look at a possible new machine involves team members in the spending decision in an empowering 'us' kind of way, that will pay off in their continuing concern about the financial performance and justification for the machine.

Similarly, a group that wrests part of its own facility's expenditure from the bland Accommodation experts cares very much how money is spent to paint the loos or fix the chairs. Maintenance, team building, and empowerment can all improve, for no additional cost at all.

Appraising Individual Performance

As we've noticed, winning is fun. Not-losing is not fun. Most formal appraisal systems are not-losing at best – dreadful and dreaded once-a-year interviews.

Managers come in all flavours, from excellent to appalling. In the hands of the best managers, any appraisal system will work wonderfully; without systems those managers (but only those) would still be telling their people how they are doing and what is expected of them. In the hands of the worst managers, any appraisal system will be stilted and useless, and their people will feel that they have had no useful feedback at all, no matter what annual rituals they have to go through and sign off.

Appraisal systems are useful for the vast majority of managers in the middle, to make them a little more rigorous about doing the slightly uncomfortable task of reviewing and feeding back on people's performance. Anything that helps the majority of managers manage better is worth supporting. So why can we not develop more human systems of appraisal!

Who Owns the Appraisal?

In most places the only 'owner' is the manager (unless it is the Personnel Department, which showers the manager with a veritable snowstorm of little notes until he has sent in his completed forms).

A few well-designed appraisal systems work for the individual as well as the organisation, to make sure both can answer the key questions:

- What do you expect of me?, and
- How am I doing?

A very few deal with the crucial question:

- What do I expect of you?

Part of the appraisal ought to highlight the employee's need for support from his own manager, and for resources, equipment, and co-ordination from other parts of the organisation. Everyone is entitled to say to the organisation: *If you want me to do a good job for you, you have to give me the tools for the task.* In the real world, the appraisal interview is one of the few opportunities people have to explore this issue with their immediate management.

Why Appraisal Systems Fail

The typical turgid, dreaded, dreadful appraisal system probably started life in perfect innocence. Then it ran into that most awful hindrance, human nature. So it developed some adaptive kinks, little 'comfort zones' to avoid embarrassment or conflict. It grew up and froze:

- The appraisal system is used to decide pay.
- The word 'appraisal' comes to mean 'the form that is filled out'.
- Employees think the appraisal system belongs to management.
- Managers think it belongs to Personnel.
- The interview happens only once a year (it would be less if both parties had their way).
- They both hide behind rigid, mechanistic scales and numbers. Nowhere is the appraiser's judgement or the appraisee's motivation part of the act.
- The manager's subjective feelings about the employee's performance are the basis for the appraisal. (It is possible to have it both ways, too subjective *and* too mechanistic, at the same time.)
- The main benefit for the employee is getting a merit award or bonus (or not), and being told that he is promotable (or not) – which completely overlooks the benefits of doing a good job now.

Physician, Heal Thyself!

A characteristic of most large organisation appraisal systems is that the higher you go up the organisation tree, the less likely it is that managers will be appraised themselves. Without good examples from the top, it is hard for the middle to see the process as anything but an uncomfortable ritual.

Annual Feedback

People want (and deserve) feedback more often than once a year.

The Perils of 'Promotability'

Appraisal often raises expectations unreasonably. In most organisations I know, at least 60 per cent of people are told they are promotable, whereas there will actually be promotions (in today's climate) for 5 per cent or less. Consider the anguish of a worker invited to take early retirement, when he has been told he is 'promotable' in every appraisal for the past ten years! Yet that is what is happening all over the industrial world today.

Blandification

Another peril in 'promotability' scoring is the natural tendency any manager has not to lose tried and trusted staff. Thus, in a typical system, anyone scored 'outstanding' gets clawed away by Human Resources for some 'development' assignment, and you have to start all over again to engage someone to cover that part of the work. On the other hand, you are stuck for ever with any employee who is scored 'unsatisfactory'. No one wants him on their team. So the safe (and most common) approach to scoring systems is to level most employees to the 'satisfactory' category (or whatever number corresponds to it), which renders the scoring system nonsense.

Performance Related Pay?

A recent IPM survey found that performance-related pay is seen by employees more as a way of managing the pay bill than as a reward for performance. Surveying more than 850 public and private sector organisations (about 20 per cent of the UK working population), IPM homed in on some interesting issues:

- There was no correlation between high performance and PRP.
- Some 75 per cent of the larger organisations (over 2500 people) had mission statements – but at least a third of these had not communicated them to employees!
- PRP was cherished by chief executives, but was a big problem for line managers – 'motivating 20 per cent of employees at the expense of the other 80 per cent'. Many reasonably competent performers need encouragement, but PRP deprives them of recognition as well as development.

- PRP is based on the individual, but works against teamwork and co-operation.
- Managers are still promoted for gung-ho problem- solving, not problem-avoiding, which is actually a key to better performance.

People who participated in PRP schemes with high expectations were finding that recession put external constraints on the rewards available, at the very time that the bureaucracy related to appraisals increased.

The organisations which did make good use of PRP were using it as part of a much wider approach to performance, looking for a performance 'culture' that would value output as well as process, and link to the service levels that 'customers' wanted.

Some Two-way Improvements

People who have a chance to decide their own measures of success will be more motivated to meeting them. Ownership is a great motivator. Obedience is just a hygiene factor.

'Productivity', for example, is something for which management is rewarded. It is not, however, always as rewarding for employees. The word either means 'Doing more,' or it means 'Doing the same, but with fewer people'. From the employees' point of view, productivity is usually 'Meeting the boss's objectives and still having time for more tea breaks'.

Negotiate Targets

Experts know that a budget that is imposed from above is less likely to be met than the one that is 'negotiated', where people have a chance to take part in the process of setting their targets. So it is with any other kind of performance.

Tough Stuff First

It takes confidence to give good feedback. You have to mix the good and bad points in a palatable recipe. You have to look someone in the eye, with respect, and say tough things in an acceptable way. Perhaps because one of my descendants is constitutionally unable to accept a compliment unless it's preceded by a complaint, I learned the effectiveness of the approach that immediately tackles all the 'bad' aspects, with a focus on the task and the remedies available, and then goes on to serious discussion of the good points, and the positive development the person expects.

Self-appraisal

If the formal appraisal is rooted in the employee's self-appraisal, the process tends to work better. Then the manager is not the judge, but a consultant. Asking questions to understand, not to educate, he or she can often suggest more positive responses, because people are usually harder on themselves than they are on others.

Peer Appraisal

A few organisations use peer appraisal to flesh out the picture generated by the employee and the manager. Peer perceptions may be useful, especially if they help build confidence. However, like the manager's perceptions, they need to be pinpointed firmly on the task. In many organisations the only recognition or reward people get for doing good work is approval and thanks from their peers.

Frequent Appraisal

Ideally, the formal appraisal machinery is backed up with good management training that makes the key elements of appraisal happen as part of the normal everyday (or everyweek) review of the work:

- compare objectives with real progress;
- discuss problems;
- adapt objectives as needed;
- review performance – focus on results;
- discuss achievement;
- look ahead: what's next?

If people give and receive this kind of 'drip-feed' there will be no surprises in the formal appraisal, simply a chance to take a longer view and discuss development.

Simpler Scoring

The good old 'pass or fail' scoring system is probably just as useful as an elaborate numbering scale. What people want to know is: 'Am I OK?' So the most a manager needs is three categories:

- Better than OK.
- OK.
- Not really OK.

I know it is heresy to suggest it, but if these 'scores' remained private between the two consenting parties, and not part of the 'personnel file', they are more likely to be honest and useful. Instead, the organisation could insist on seeing the development outcome, or training plan, for each employee after each formal appraisal.

The Development Payoff

It is perfectly possible to harness individual and team perform-ance feedback to individual and team development. In fact, it is only when appraisal leads clearly to development and training that the manager, the employee and the organisation can all win – and be seen to win.

A number of organisations move the appraiser around the table to scan the organisation with the appraisee for development opportunities. This is where the employee can say: 'I've been doing the Open University management course, and I'd like to become more involved on the planning side.' Or the manager might offer: 'We've been looking at a project that could make use of your computer skills. Are you interested in learning more about spreadsheets?' There is a big difference here between a 'development plan' (which may be rather vague, depending on outside opportunities to come to fruition), and a 'training plan', which simply lists (and, one hopes, schedules) courses that fill specific needs or wants.

Pick-and-mix Appraisal Script

Many managers are initially shy about discussing people's performance; they tend to utter platitudes, and sigh with relief when the session is over. The answer is to use the facts, and ask for facts. The more people feel they can review their own performance, the better it works.

In the hands of the excellent manager, the following is probably unnecessary, and in the hands of the bad manager, it will probably not help. But for the many managers in between, a 'script' may help. Carol Milne at the Royal Infirmary of Edinburgh drew my attention to the following Role Conversation,[1] which may be useful for both participants.

The first stage is the two participants agreeing and listing a set of objectives or key tasks they expect to be achieved within the period. Then they draw up a performance plan:

- Actions: Who will do what and when?
- Outcomes: How will the objectives be measured?
- Opportunities: What can help the employee achieve the objectives?
- Constraints: What will limit achievement of the objectives?
- Revisions: Any agreed modifications (with date and reasons).

Ideally, the employee could be in the lead in all this conversation, but in the real world it is probably difficult for managers to let go the reins. After 4–6 months, the two schedule another formal meeting to undertake the Role Conversation, and modify some of the objectives or key tasks as necessary. Both review the Role Conversation form before their discussion.

Although the Role Conversation uses a lot of paper (each topic is listed on a single page, with plenty of room for comments), it gives both manager and managed a safe structure for their discussion, with minimum bureaucracy, but review at a higher level to assure that it is done fairly.

Activities of my job
What do I see as the key activities of my job?
What does my manager see as my key activities?

What do my junior colleagues see as my key activities?
What are the most frustrating aspects?

My time
To which activities do I give the most time?
Is this the allocation of time I would like?
Is it what my manager would like?

My commitment
Which parts of my job interest me most?
Which parts of my job interest me least?
How does this affect the way I do my job?

Resources: time, money, space, equipment
What significant resources do I manage?
In what ways are these deficient?
How could I manage them better?

Employees (including the grade and/or number)
What employees do I manage?
What are their strengths/areas requiring development?
How could I manage them better?

Procedures and systems
What procedures and systems do I initiate/modify/maintain?
Do others approve/discourage/complain about these?
If they complain, what is their complaint?
Do I have difficulty getting others to implement these systems?
What systems do I dislike?
Why?
What formal reporting do I have to do?
What formal reporting do I expect from others?

Relationship with my senior manager
How much time do I spend a week with my senior manager?
Would I like more or less?
What is the nature of contact, advice, information, guidance?
Would I like this changed?
Why?
How does my manager judge me?
What does he/she think of me and my work?
What are the things which bring blame/praise?
Is my manager open about his/her feelings towards me?

Relationship with junior staff

How much time do I spend a week with my staff?
Do I spend more time with some than others?
Why?
How do staff feel about the frequency of meetings?
What is the nature of our contact?
How do I judge them? Am I open about my feelings?
What do they feel about me as a manager?
How often do I give them feedback on their performance?
Do I do work which they should be doing?
If so, what, and why?

Policies

Are there any policies I do not understand?
Are there any policies I do not agree with?
How do the attitudes of others in the unit affect the way I work?
How is the unit managed (openness, supportive, leadership style and so on)?

Individual

What am I good at? My own skills and areas of competence?
Would my manager and others agree?
What situations cause me problems?
Am I content and motivated by my job? (Be specific about the good and less-good aspects)
How do I think I am doing? (Be specific about the good and less-good aspects)

This process

This conversation has been . . . (how useful?) (How could it be improved – questions added or excluded?)

At the end of the conversation, the participants prioritise the employee's development needs for (1) knowledge (e.g. techniques, theories, processes); (2) skills or competences (i.e. demonstrably doing things well); and (3) desirable attitudes. I have reservations about including the third item, as it may turn the process back into a management-driven, parent-child relationship, and it probably does not actually do anything to improve attitudes on either side.

The next output is an *action plan*:

- As a result of this conversation I will do the following:
- My manager will do the following:

The manager completes a one-page *Summary of Discussion*, including space for the post-holder's comments. This is also signed off by the reviewer, usually the manager's boss, who also signs off the *Record of Performance*, which lists the objectives, with comments on their achievement.

Group-generated Performance Measures

Teams, like individuals, are entitled to know where they stand. The prerequisite to any kind of performance focus is a clear knowledge of what is expected of them. For many managers this can happen naturally through regular team meetings that review the team's performance.

Charles Margerison[2] postulates a relatively elaborate team appraisal process, in which each member of the team receives everyone else's initial personal self-appraisal form (not the version containing the manager's comments). They then hold a group meeting to look at how individual team members have helped or hindered others in achieving team objectives, and actions that can be taken to improve teamwork. The team leader writes up the outcomes of the team appraisal, and manages the team and its members along the agreed guidelines.

This is a useful process, but only in the hands of capable and confident supervisors. If they are that good, I would hope they could go further, towards a more adult team relationship aiming at group-generated performance information. Energy can be directed and performance improved, to everyone's benefit, if a group, just like an individual, has a chance to understand and discuss some basic questions:

- Where are we now?
- Where do we want to go – and why?
- How are we going to get there?
- How do we know when we're winning?

Group-generated performance reports can actually help improve performance. This touches on 'voluntary' energy, and in that sense is delicate, demanding nurture combined with tact. The power to direct rests with the manager, but the benefit comes from the added value people can contribute when they are motivated, looking for ways to win.

Thus, you can set up a system for groups to discuss their own performance but, once again, only the groups that actually feel they 'own' the process will perform better as a result. Rather than an elaborate system, I should like to see more emphasis on management development (and a little training) to generate supervisors and middle managers who can use this tool effectively.

The first question is what the group wants to measure. Next, they decide how to go about it. Once the agreed measurement data comes into group meetings they have a basis to decide what improvements are practical. If it develops properly, the process begins to work in the manner shown in Figure 15.1.

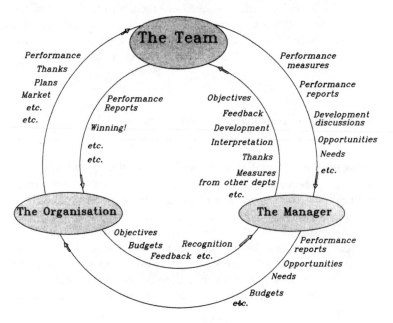

Figure 15.1 Performance Reporting Cycle

The ideal manager will launch the process, give his team regular feedback on what is expected – and keep his hands off their decisions. Only after several months of trial-and-error, when measures are fairly well established but not set in concrete, is it useful to question the measures. Silence is golden – if the group doesn't own the process, it won't work.

As measures develop, the manager can interpret the organisation's performance, and that of divisions or departments, in terms that make sense of the team's measures, and show how the team is contributing. 'Every time you win on this one, George says Final Assembly's measures drop. Is there a way you can do this so that both groups can win?'

Just as the individual should be able to use the appraisal process to review the resources he needs to do his job properly, the team should be able to use performance reporting to let management know what they need in order to perform even better.

This is a temptation, of course; some will inevitably turn their wits to embellishing the real needs, which is part of the fun for them. Frequently, however, what a team feels it needs is in the best interests of the organisation: less bureaucracy here, better information there, some just-in-time thinking, or doing things right first time.

Matching Management Measures

Performance information from teams as well as individuals can be used to develop and steer the organisation more effectively, but only when everyone understands and respects another law: *Performance belongs to the performer.*

The organisation that aspires to invert its triangle, to empower its people, can gain benefits by asking for and respecting their group performance reports. When performance information about individuals and groups is flowing properly (that means two ways, regularly, face to face, credibly) the organisation wins in a number of ways.

Shared Direction

Clear goals mean focused management, and performance reporting puts a natural 'task' orientation into people's work. Counter-productive 'office politics' can be minimised.

Structure and Monitoring

Because managers have structures to support their good intentions, the information about the organisation's goals flows easily and regularly.

Planning

Employees can see the logic in the corporate plans, because the plans relate to day-to-day performance, and the planners gain quantifiable data about how the organisation works.

Well-trained Resources

Managers can plan the training that individuals and groups need to meet specified standards and to develop the business of the organisation.

Flexibility

Regular performance review means that people can change direction in unison as soon as they see reasons for it. Spotting and clarifying those reasons is part of good management.

To achieve all this, of course, the managers themselves need constant training and retraining in ways to appraise and encourage performance reporting

Notes

1. The Role Conversation was developed at the Management Development Group of the Scottish Health Service some years ago.

2. Charles Margerison (1991), 'Improving and Reviewing Performance,' in *Making Management Development Work: Achieving Success in the Nineties*, Maidenhead: McGraw-Hill.

16

Training for Empowerment

Not all people are ready for empowerment at the same time or in the same way. Both empowering managers and empowerable employees require time to get used to the idea. People who have been hostages take a long time to adjust to freedom, and the same holds for organisational hostages, whose whole lives have been constrained in little boxes, just as much as for political prisoners.

Motivation to Learn

Freedom can be a threat as well as a promise. Particularly among managers some will feel that empowering those below is going to disempower those higher up. Others worry that it will reveal their own or their subordinates' shortcomings or 'lack of ability'. I believe that 'lack of ability' is a myth, but I have to respect the number of people who worry about it.

Empowering people is not a skill or a 'competence' that you learn in the classroom. It is a strategy for the organisation, and a personal conviction for the manager. The strategy needs to be spelled out so clearly that managers are at least aware of what is expected of them. It is safe to assume that few managers in the middles of large organisations feel naturally committed to empowering. When the strategy and the conviction diverge, the organisation needs to respect the manager's reservations – and look for ways to help real conviction develop and mature.

One way to learn the benefits of empowerment is to spend some time in a non-threatening place where people are more empowered; action-learning approaches to management development can offer this benefit. A manager can absorb different approaches without any risk when he or she is not in the normal environment.

Some organisations use 'sheep-dip', rapid immersion of the entire flock for an inspirational day or so (at most). I have grave reservations about the sheep-dip approach to empowerment or any other change model, for management or for troops, on several counts:

- It raises expectations that cannot usually be met.
- The training is interesting but relevance may be low, or else highly relevant projects are identified and planned, but no time is allowed for their completion in the following weeks or months.
- Employees see huge amounts of money being spent on something that seems peripheral to their real tasks.
- The result of sheep-dip training is usually increased management lip-service, thus creating more cynics.

As we saw in Chapter 14 on team meetings I prefer the 'sheep dog' model – a robust change manager who can credibly coach supervisors, feed back unpopular perceptions to top managers, and arrange the right training for teams and individuals as soon as they perceive the need for it, but not before.

Training professionals have batteries of tests, most of which seem devised to establish the subject's weaknesses. There is a prevalent belief that the purpose of training is to find out what you are bad at and then train you until you come up to par.

This belies everything I know about human motivation! What motivates people generally is what they are *good* at. If the tests were used to discover people's *strengths* and then develop them some more, what a turn-on it would be. Given that approach to development, they may even feel confident enough to fill some of those gaps themselves.

Action-learning Approaches: a problem is an opportunity

The classroom is not always the best place in which to learn work skills, particularly the arts of management. The organisation itself is a very effective laboratory.

Some of the best training is based on problem-solving, individually or in groups. Team projects can create great momentum for their members, and some pleasant surprises for their managers. People with experience in Quality Circles and Quality Improvement Teams recognise how creative any normal group of employees can be when they have a few tools for analysis and a charter to tackle problems within their own sphere. A manager needs to respect his or her employees before he can begin to empower them. Managing quality projects may be an important prerequisite to managing empowerment,

Reg Revans is a management thinker and activist, a veteran of those heady post-war years in the National Coal Board. Recognising the limitations of the classroom, he developed an approach called 'action learning' to help adults learn with and from each other. In its purest form, the manager from the steel mill tackles a banking problem, the personnel specialist works on a marketing problem. A number of supporting mechanisms make sure that the participants implement solutions as well as recommending them:

- A co-consulting 'project set' with perhaps half a dozen fellow participants. They meet together often enough and long enough to care about each other's projects.
- A 'set adviser' who facilitates, brings in experts on demand, and makes sure the participants reflect on and learn from their own experience and each other's.
- A sponsoring manager who owns the problem the participant

is tackling – ideally a problem that entails crossing boundaries and dealing with power and organisational politics.
- A mentor or boss who has a vested interest in the participant's development.

This structure can be long term and elaborate, or quite informal and easy. Members can deal with their own problems or each other's, full time, part time or sporadically. Extra energy comes from the set meeting checkpoint, the fact you have to report progress to the other members, and the challenge to learn as well as take action.

A group of individuals can meet as a project set to tackle their own or each other's problems. In its simplest form, teams or individuals can compete for project awards, and top management can fuel the development by recognising excellence wherever it occurs.

Deep-end Development

The best way to develop leaders is to throw them in at the deep end. A quick survey of members of any course will show 'deep-end' experiences: 'My boss broke his leg'; 'I had to take over the Indonesia office'; 'We had to get the product to market faster'. These events far outweigh formal training as turning-points in people's careers.

Most organisations do deep-end development inadvertently. Some would-be managers simply sink; others learn and then leave. To make the most of deep-end development, the organisation needs to send them in with some form of water-wings.

This is where the mentor comes in. When the people who become mentors are known for empowering skills, it is fairly easy to add mentoring skills. Like the action-learning set adviser, the formal or informal mentor needs to help the person who has been thrown in at the deep end to learn from the perplexities he or she is facing.

One well-known management centre was planning a high-profile course in supervisory skills a few years ago. Then the planners asked some supervisors what skills they needed. Most of the responses concerned the first few weeks on the new job; and the knowledge the new supervisors needed was already inside the organisation: how to fill out this form, what to do about discipline, and so on. Instead of teaching supervision, the management centre developed a successful course on how to mentor new supervisors.

Taking Responsibility

Scottish consultant Rob Wilmot was involved with a project to redesign the work of British Airways baggage supervisors a few years ago. Disempowered supervisors felt they had no power to change anything. The supervisors were offered a chance to help develop a different job, then spell out the powers they would need to do it. They looked at the whole sequence of support and development and assessment. The managers above them were brought in as mentors and made responsible for the supervisors achieving the assessment standards they had helped specify.

An important part of the BA change programme was joint setting of achievable targets. By lowering unrealistic targets the company began to obtain better performance! This change involved 2500 people, all with new roles, and was implemented within eleven months. From the customer's point of view, empowering the supervisors made the baggage arrive faster.

Getting busy managers in the middle to mentor sometimes demands an autocratic voice from higher management. In the long run, it is good for the mentoring manager, and very good for the person being developed.

Just-in-time Training

There is nothing wrong with traditional training, except that it tends to be dealt out in portions convenient to the trainer at times that suit the giver, not the recveivers. During one period of rapid change and work pressure the front-line managers in one large company were being shepherded through Dale Carnegie, Put the

Customer First, the ABCs of Budgeting, Total Quality Management, Tom Peters' Excellence, and one or two local initiatives. They were virtually trainer-proof!

Those same people actually asked for some training after they dived in at the deep end and tried to hold two-way team meetings. Without techniques and some tricks to manage the process, they knew they were floundering. A helpful coach offered some intimate, practical workshops that filled the gap once the supervisors recognised their own need.

This may be called the map-of-Madrid syndrome – good map; big city, but I do not need the map until I am actually standing outside the Prado wondering which way I have to turn to get to my hotel. That's when I begin to value the map and pay attention to it.

Nate Newkirk developed some interesting technical training for Xerox in the early 1970s. He took the best repair person they had for a particular machine, stood her in front of a class, and announced:

> This is Sadie; she knows everything there is to know about this copier. But Sadie doesn't like to talk much, so here are the manuals, and each of you has a stripped-down machine to work on. You can ask Sadie anything you like, but you'll have to ask it in a way she can answer 'yes' or 'no'.

Those people learned just as well as their counterparts in more traditional classrooms, but a year later they recalled twice as much. When they had to work out the questions for themselves, they valued the answers.

DIY Development

To empower people it helps if they believe they control some of the use of their time. Some organisations say: 'Five per cent is your own.' That is, for a quarter of a day the individual should have free time within his work to do whatever he fancies towards self-development.

Giving people time to develop themselves works outside, as

well as inside an organisation. IBM and Xerox (among others) openly encourage any employee anywhere in the world to take up to 10 per cent of their work time for outside activities they care about, with a supervisor's permission. But woe unto the supervisor who says no, because those companies have well-oiled 'open door' grievance procedures. Those companies do not, however, lighten a person's workload, even by 1 per cent, much less ten. They just use the old adage: 'If you want something done, ask a busy person to do it.'

If people do not feel empowered and involved inside work, they will pour their abilities and enthusiasms somewhere outside. If you ask people what they do outside work, you discover how much ability the organisation is probably failing to tap. Here is an opera singer, there is a croupier, there is a father driving his daughter 40 miles every night to practise for the Olympics, here is a JP, there is an Open University student.

If an organisation can encourage its people, especially frontline managers, to take up outside responsibilities, real management learning can result. People who are able to manage volunteers, for example, will understand more about leadership than MBA graduates who have never had this development opportunity.

Outside volunteer activity can be a turning-point for a younger manager. Projects like the Duke of Edinburgh's scheme, with activities in the community for school students, succeed because they develop skills in managing and empowering people, as well as the joy of exercising them for something worthwhile.

I recall a 'DIY Degree' started a few years ago at North East London Polytechnic (now the University of East London) when Ian Cunningham was there. I used to think of it as 'the lorry-driver's degree'. Building on some of Revans' action learning ideas, a programme was set up for about 20 adults who came from a variety of backgrounds, without the 'O' and 'A' levels required for normal entry. They spent quite a long time working with an adviser to define what they wanted to learn about, and how they would know if they had learned it. For instance, a pre-retirement foreman wanted to learn Gaelic, Irish History, Farming Methods and Small Business Principles, so that he could go back to Connemara and restore his uncle's run-down farm.

The measures the students negotiated ranged from passing

specified exams or writing papers to doing projects on which they would be judged.

The action-learning aspects of the programme brought people together in groups once a fortnight, to tell each other (and a 'set adviser') how they were getting on, and as time went on a kind of 'co-consulting' developed. The set adviser acted more as facilitator and broker than expert, identifying whatever pertinent know-how lurked in various parts of the college, or outside it, and making sure that people took every opportunity to reflect on their experience and learn from it.

This is not a bad model for the manager as developer (which is my preferred model for the 'manager as appraiser'). It rests on the assumption that people are adult, that they want development, that they will work hard to achieve it.

A useful product based on Revans' concept is the First-Line Manager (FLM) package available from Henley Distance Learning. This innovative package is intended for groups of supervisors with an inside or outside adviser, working over about a year. Without lectures, essays, or other academic props, they gain Level 4 management qualifications. FLM is based on a rigorously structured set of books that lead the members of the group through a comprehensive process. Bit by bit, project by project, they gain knowledge, competence and confidence, working with their peers and their teams to solve real, practical problems in their work. The structure involves their immediate managers at every stage, as well as a more senior sponsoring manager. The end result is proof, measurable, assessable, quantifiable, in the form of the completed books and the completed year of project set meetings, that the 'student' has mastered high-level management concepts.

Qualifications are nevertheless important, (especially to their holders!). I do not for a moment question the value of an MBA, a DMS, an 'O' level, an IPM certificate, or any other qualification. People work hard for their qualifications, and deserve respect and encouragement as a result.

On the other hand, especially in large organisations, specifying qualifications for jobs often replaces the exercise of good judgement! People feel 'safer' trusting a known qualification, though for many jobs the qualifications are meaningless! I recall a manager with a first at Cambridge who was constitutionally unable to 'manage' anything. He did not administer, he could not manage people, and he did not make decisions – but he was wonderful at tracking the organisation's culture and relating it to events in Ancient Greece! He was also a fine resource about protocol, and the history of the organisation, but the only way the organisation could deal with his qualification was to make him a manager. Remember the Belbin team-role results. The same person, with the same qualifications, can be a winner in one team, and a loser in another, because the composition and focus of the team is such an important aspect of success.

The best basis for decisions about an individual is performance. If people know what is expected of them, they will develop the competence they need to achieve it.

17

The Survey as Organisational Tin-opener

If you want to empower people, ask them how. If you want to underscore how disempowered they are, ask them a lot of questions about things that you will not or cannot change as a result of their answers. To put this in the form of a law:

If you're going to change things, ask people first.

This carries a corollary:

Don't ask about things you can't change.

IBM is entitled to ask its people their impressions of their management, their pay and perks, their personnel policies, even their products: the IBM people have a history of more than 20 years of surveys that resulted in changes they could see. Very few other companies I know would adjust such intimate artifacts as pay in response to insider perceptions.

The Benefits of Surveys

An employee survey is an increasingly popular way of asking people in an organisation what they think about it. Surveys can range from one page with a few questions on it to many pages and many questions. They can be voluntary, done in the employee's own time, or more supervised, where people are shepherded into rooms set aside for the purpose. A survey can go to everyone, or just a sample.

Surveying people can add energy. A good survey can be a tin-opener, bringing out things that have been hidden, starting the dialogue. A survey offers a number of advantages for managers involved in bringing about change:

- It increases management awareness and understanding of how their people feel, all the way from front-line management to the top.
- You start with confidence about where you are.
- People are pleased to be asked – as long as they believe it will lead to appropriate action.
- Myths, fables and truisms can be tested.
- Hidden trouble spots become visible, and difficult issues can be opened up in a non-threatening way.
- It is natural and easy to start people talking about where they want to be, and how to get there.
- You can develop a 'map' of management credibility in different parts of the organisation.
- You acquire benchmarks or yardsticks for measuring change, in directions you specify by asking about them.
- You get early warning of looming issues – as you go on you can see changes in perceptions.
- Policies and strategies are better-rooted – the 'art of the possible' is encouraged.
- Management gains information to manage the business better.

Some people use surveys mainly to reveal hotspots before they turn into strikes. In my view, if you have to wait for the annual or bi-annual survey to spot a danger, you are in trouble already.

Any sensible organisation has more immediate and responsive hotspot-sensing, like listening to their own supervisors or shop stewards.

To me the most important use of surveys is to light the fuse, then to monitor how change is progressing. The following chapters include considerable detail about how BT and IBM have used surveys, along with other communication mechanisms. Many other companies are developing highly professional surveys and administering them well. A pick-and-mix survey is included in the resources section at the end of the book.

In a small group the best way to survey is to ask people, face to face, what they think about an issue. You can discuss it on the spot, individually or in groups, and begin to plan action immediately. That is responsive management.

In larger organisations, you need ways to get the same responsive 'feel'. Various survey methods are available: face-to-face interviews, phone interviews, group discussions, postal questionnaires, questionnaires completed in supervised groups, questionnaires cascaded down through the management line, and so on.

Survey Mechanics

One of the best (and potentially least expensive) ways to ask a large number of people about something is to generate a short, simple questionnaire and make sure that everyone receives one. If everyone believes the answers will be truly anonymous, at least half send it back, and you then summarise the results and tell them all what they said.

There are other ways: (*a*) ask a smaller sample; (*b*) generate a long, sophisticated questionnaire; (*c*) leave the distribution to normal channels or the house magazine; (*d*) offer prizes for good answers; (*e*) do without the uncomfortable feedback meetings and just publish a few paragraphs in the house magazine; (*f*) give everyone all the responses to everything. I have reservations about all of these.

Sampling

If you use sampling, you are only involving a 'representative' proportion of people. When the results are published, only those who filled out the questionnaires are going to be really interested. Worse, the managers whose weak points are revealed can dismiss the sampling as flawed – 'That's not what most of my people think.' On the other hand, sampling ought to cost less.

Elaborate Questionnaires

If you have a long questionnaire, you probably *have* to send it to fewer people, because of the expense of processing all the responses. You pay by the question, by the number of responses. Once you have computers and automatic reading equipment and special pencils involved, your cost for the survey rises steeply and it takes longer. But once you have tried a survey and decided to repeat it regularly for a very large number of people, this may be the best approach. One international company went so far down the 'management by questionnaire' line it developed a monster survey asking people's perceptions on physical working conditions, workload and hours, pay, benefits, views of local, national and international management, job security, plans to stay, company advertising, community involvement, product competitiveness, and employee talents. *This sort of headquarters peering-over-the-shoulder disempowers managers!*

House Magazine Distribution

If survey distribution is left to 'normal' channels you may be wasting time, effort and money, unless you are certain your normal channels are near perfect. One organisation spent a great deal of money to survey 3000 employees, but received only 200 responses. Why? The forms were sent to departments stapled to the back of the normal (relatively boring) newsletter – and everyone knew the enclosures at the back were even more boring. Very few of the employees even found the wretched survey.

Prizes

There is no evidence that offering people prizes to submit their views increases either their confidence or management's credibility. Quite the reverse! It is insulting to people who care about the issues, and you cannot have both prizes and anonymous responses.

Feedback Famine

As to feedback – without that, there is little sense in doing a survey! I know senior managers who want to survey their people simply from vicarious interest, or because the company next door did it. These are the people who are most likely to stick the results in the bottom left-hand drawer of the desk when the survey returns some less than flattering comments or lower than expected results.

Feedback Flood

The opposite situation is just as bad – what might be called 'Snow them with data!' Surveys generate a great deal of data. People (especially managers and even more especially survey 'owners') deserve to have the reams interpreted sensibly, in terms that everyone can understand. I remember one ponderous national survey, the first a large company had ever conducted, which resulted in a 400-page bound tome of computer-printed numbers going out to every key manager in the field, with no explanation whatsoever. One manager (himself an excellent statistician) took his volume home to try to make sense of it. While he put off the dreaded task, his Irish wolfhound found a better use for 400 pages of numbers: she used it as a teething ring, until a good chunk was shredded pulp. And that is exactly what that form of survey report deserves! The feedback, not the questionnaire, is the tin-opener. We shall return to this point shortly.

Potential Pitfalls

Trust is inevitably one of the things you are trying to measure

when you survey people, yet most of the surveys that fail have
problems with regard to trust.

Employee Distrust

If they don't believe their management, they won't believe
assurances of anonymity, and they won't fill out a questionnaire.
On the first occasion (and in some companies every occasion),
people need a sealed envelope and even a 'safe' address before
they will believe their responses are going to be anonymous.
Until employees see action as a result of someone asking their
perceptions, they will distrust management's motives.

Union Distrust

In some circumstances (usually when a survey has been sprung
on them without prior discussion), unions may worry that the
survey is supplanting agreed consultative procedures. In most
cases the unions have already been trying to highlight some of
the concerns management wants to tackle (like poor communication with employees), and they could be quite helpful in
framing the questions and ensuring that feedback is well
regarded.

Management Distrust

I have known surveys to be frozen out by managers and
supervisors who suspect no benefits and many drawbacks –
especially if *they* have not been consulted in advance. The more
that managers are involved in setting the questions, the more
likely they are to help respond to the answers.

Secrecy

This is an associated problem. Especially the first time an
organisation is surveyed, its managers naturally worry about the
results. Unless they have to *promise feedback from the start*, they
would prefer to temporise about what will happen after the
survey. Surveys gather dust in bottom drawers for several
normal and natural (but not very nice) reasons:

- Uncertainty – we don't know what to do with all this;
- Power – data with which to win internal jousts;
- Preconceptions – 'Don't disturb me with facts!'

The organisation should have no secrets, but the privacy of its members must be respected. This need for guaranteed confidentiality is the main reason I recommend using an outsider to process the survey, at least for the first time. It is not to do with skills and techniques (though those are useful, and easily transferred inside); it is to do with the credibility of the survey and people's belief in its confidentiality.

Ownership

An unowned survey will never work. It has been known for a progressive manager inside a large organisation to be transferred, just as his people have expressed themselves, tentatively but honestly, for the first time, in response to his invitation. The only solution for this disaster recipe is to make sure that any successor has sworn on a huge stack of bibles to pick up the torch and respect the responses.

An ambivalent owner? Many suffer mixed feelings, and with some justification. Hearing what people think can be uncomfortable. Change is usually uncomfortable. Learning is usually uncomfortable. But the commitment that launched the survey needs to be kept together long enough to begin to gain some of the rewards.

Inside or Outside?

Especially where there are questions of trust, it is not always wise to run your first survey from inside. An outsider can be seen to be fair, impartial, and not susceptible to massaging data or hiding unpleasant results. The manager who is sufficiently trusted to run a survey does not need a survey to tell him what his people think. But in a large organisation, is he the exception or the rule? DIY is not usually the best way to find out, nor the first time. After people have seen things improve, they will probably be more survey-wise and the second time around might well be managed by a trusted insider.

The Consultant Glut

At the other end of this spectrum is the overoiled machinery of huge surveys and specialist jargon. 'Qualitative' or 'quantitative' surveys, for example, just mean 'with numbers' or 'without numbers'. (If you want it 'without', they put much of the report in quotation marks, and what they cannot extract verbatim they make up or paraphrase.) Survey consultants tend to talk too much about 'the confidence limits of data', assorted sampling techniques, and questionnaire construction.

Overdoing It

A manager who has worked hard to improve the performance that lagged in survey responses will want another survey right away to show (or check) how well he is doing. Resist the temptation! Credibility takes a long time to take root, and uprooting this delicate plant to see how it is doing will harm it. Most surveys should not take place more often than once a year, unless you have built a culture where people are accustomed to being asked specific questions fairly regularly. Even there, give change a chance! The manager who wants to see his progress has a better means at his disposal: *go out and ask people in person*. The chance to discuss progress and see the manager's interest and commitment can be very positive when people are already perceiving change in response to their comments.

League Table Laggards

The survey can help create and reinforce new values, especially through the league tables of managers who are living up to them in the eyes of their subordinates. This aspect is useful but has certain pitfalls:

- The survey should generate a number of league tables, not a single list of 'good guys and bad guys'. It should help managers improve their strong points as well as improve their weaknesses, in the eyes of their people.
- The survey should focus on the task, not the manager's personality or 'niceness'. The 'score your manager' surveys

that are sometimes conducted tend to ignore this, unless they ask people how their boss does various tasks. A company full of unfocused but popular managers is not going to fulfil the expectations of its board or its employees.

Rules of Thumb

Starting a survey is like starting a baby. It may seem effortless, but once you have started, you have created an obligation – and, like the baby, it can only grow. Once you ask people to tell you, in confidence, what they really feel, you are obliged to take notice.

1. A survey must be owned.
2. Start where you want to finish: a good survey offers its owner few surprises, but many tools.
3. Let everybody know when it is coming, and why.
4. Ask about the things people care about: the organisation's climate and culture, employee communications content and channels, management credibility, perceptions of policies and customers, the work itself, development and training.
5. Do not ask about the things managers cannot influence: pay and benefits, corporate policy, and the like (unless the survey is actually going to be used to review them – in which case, say so). Following this principle, why ask about the age and sex of employees? The query can seem to threaten confidentiality, and Personnel should already know the make-up of the workforce.
6. Give full feedback. Print the feedback promise on the questionnaire. In a typical communication survey people will tell you by which channels they want the findings to reach them (usually face to face).
7. Assure privacy by restricting specific group feedback to clusters where there were 20 or more responses. (Some large companies with established surveys can retain trust with a limit of 10, but 20 is safer.) Where fewer than 20 people in a group responded, their results can be consolidated together with others in the larger element.

Getting Started

Before you start, everybody needs to know why the survey is being done, what is going to happen, how, how the material is going to be used, and when and how the results will come back to them. This is the appropriate time to ask managers (and trade union people) what issues they would like to see in the survey.

The owner will probably need a steering group, to spread awareness and help look at the issues, the distribution, and the feedbacks. Sometimes an appropriate group already exists, but this is usually an opportunity to add momentum to change and make sure that there are people monitoring the results.

Distribution can test the normal communication links, as long as you plan in ways to pick up missing people. Often headquarters will have more confidence in its computer systems than do people out on the line. One way to test is to print individual names on the cover letters (*not* on survey forms!), and distribute via heads of departments, giving each a few spare copies and directions to send in corrections.

If you are using a consultant, you need to plan a cover letter from the chairman or managing director that explains that the results are going direct to the consultant, ensure that individual responses are handled off-site, and that only summary information comes back.

Fast Feedback!

You've promised it. Now deliver.

The more questions you asked, the more complicated the data is going to be. For managers as well as troops, it is important to simplify, yet everyone will want to feel that the full results have been revealed, (one more argument for the short, simple questionnaire!). Bar graphs are usually easiest to understand, though you must make sure that all responses are shown to the same scale. Desktop computers manage this kind of data pretty decently.

If you invite write-in comments they need to be summarised,

yet also to be typed up verbatim. People need to be assured that their own observations have been taken into account. I usually publish comments from each department only in that department's report, to keep the overall report brief, yet meet the local needs.

Every question needs full analysis. There will be a 'league table' for each question. It is up to the 'owner' to decide which subjects are most important, and how the general responses are going to be published. I feel it is very important for any employee to be able to go and look at the detailed data.

If you asked people to say what department they are in, they deserve to see what their department responded. One way to simplify this is to generate the figures for the whole organisation, and also for each division or unit. If you have data for departments within those units, print graphs of the organisation and unit results, with space for the department or sub-unit managers to graph in their own results, question by question. That adds to their sense of owning the data.

It can take several weeks for the replies to be returned, unless you gather people on company time to complete the form (an approach that negates the response rate as a measure of morale or credibility – anything less than 100 per cent just shows poor monitoring). I prefer a less schoolmarm-ish approach: leaving it to employees to fill out the form when and where they choose.

People will be most interested in the results while they still recall filling out the form, so fast response is important. Ideally, the top team reviews the findings, including league tables of divisions or units, and then the division or unit management repeats the process. Each level 'owns' the comparative data from one layer down, but employees and their managers may prefer to feel that their own data is not available to higher management unless the 'owners' choose to show it to them.

You can graph a cluster of questions together, or a cluster of responses to a single question. Both are useful. Figure 17.1 is based on a cluster of questions about the work itself, which is fed back to a department head or even to an individual front-line manager and his team. It compares their results with that of the organisation as a whole. The keywords in this instance stand for the following statements:

The work itself
How Finance people responded

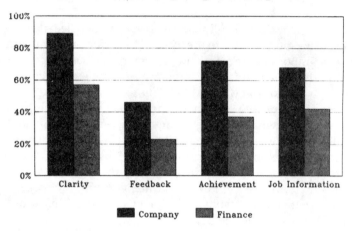

Figure 17.1 Single Group, Compared with the Organisation

- Clarity: 'I am quite clear what is expected of me.'
- Feedback: 'I get enough information to know how well I am doing.'
- Achievement: 'My work gives me a feeling of achievement.'
- Job information: 'I have the information I need to do my job well.'

Clustering the responses like this usually highlights a close correlation between performance feedback and the sense of achievement.

This kind of chart, illustrated in Figure 17.2, is particularly useful to encourage groups that have worked hard to improve poor survey results in a previous period, or to highlight parts of the organisation where survey feedback has been stifled or ignored.

Figure 17.3 uses a vertical bar chart to compare what six different groups in a unit felt about a single question (dealing with their managers' style). By emphasising the percentage who agreed with the statement 'Most of the time it is safe to say what

The work itself
How Finance people responded

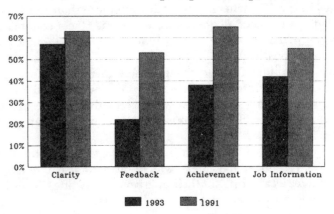

Figure 17.2 Single Group, Compared with Own Responses in Earlier Year

Supervisors give recognition
1993 responses by department

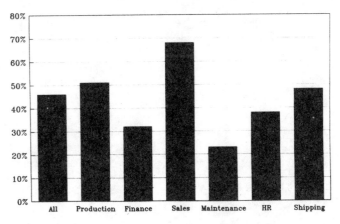

Figure 17.3 Several Groups, Single Question

you think' the graph creates a very clear league table, and helps reinforce a value for openness.

Finance, Works and Admin showed lower levels of trust, with scores in the 30s, whereas in Production more than 50 per cent agreed. A year later all groups were over the 50 per cent mark – and the managers were paying more attention to employees' need to be heard.

I try to limit feedback to groups where there were 20 or more responses, to protect people's sense of privacy. And for the manager who says, 'I know who wrote that comment', the answer is always: 'Several people wrote it. It doesn't matter who wrote it. Is it true?'

Once they have taken part in a review meeting at the more senior level, most managers will be able to use the graphs themselves as a 'script' for their own review meetings. They and their people are interested in several aspects:

- Where are we doing better than average? Why?
- Where are we doing worse than average? Why?
- What are we going to do differently as a result?

Part III

Empowerment in Action

The case studies in Part III demonstrate different approaches to managing empowerment in very large organisations.

The somewhat paternal IBM model suffered terrible stresses as the company released 70,000 people in 1990–1, another 40,000 in 1992, and about 25,000 in 1993. More than 100,000 were scheduled to go by the end of 1994. After 80 years, IBM had to scrap its famous 'full employment policy', the job security promise that had always underpinned much of the company's personnel policy. This was an aspect of modern management that the Japanese studied and began to emulate in the 1950s.

BT, streamlining through a period of profit, had to make clear to its employees why early retirement for 30,000 was necessary in 1992, with ongoing ads thereafter. Though the company had never had compulsory redundancy, it had always shied away from making any 'for ever' promises.

IBM's intensive employee communications and brilliant use of its own high technology certainly helped to keep people informed, but the internal excellence may actually have induced a smugness that made the company impervious to external trends.

The BT model, concentrating on employee communication, was derived over a shorter period, perhaps a little more haphazardly. With a history of market dominance and control that is just as vulnerable as IBM's, it will be interesting to see how BT deals with the outside world in the next few years.

18

IBM: High-tech Empowerment for Tough Times

IBM reported losses of nearly $5 billion for 1992, on sales of $64 billion – the largest annual loss ever reported in the USA. The loss actually included $11.6 billion set aside to pay for restructuring (and letting people go). This was after rather large write-offs for restructuring in the preceding three years. By 1993 IBM shocked observers by showing a similar $5 billion loss for a single quarter. Britain in the 1992 recession was one of the blackest spots in the IBM world, reporting operating losses of almost £400 million, with a restructuring charge of £218 million.

IBM's loss was as large as the GNP of a smaller country, just as for many years IBM's profits were often compared with other countries' GNP. That should concentrate the mind wonderfully! Just as it had been a model in good times, perhaps IBM will be another kind of model for hard times.

IBM has some of the finest long-range forecasting in the world, but in December 1992 chairman John Akers had to write to shareholders that bad news was coming:

Since October, the sharp decline in our European business has continued, with no immediate sign of improvement. The Japanese economic environment is weakening, and results in IBM Japan are under pressure. The outlook for our North American operations has not improved. The depth of these downturns was not anticipated.

Not only employee job security but also the shareholders' sacred dividend had to suffer. When IBM cut the quarterly dividend from $1.54 to $.54 in early 1993 Akers announced his resignation. For the first time in history, the company went outside, and even outside the industry, to find his successor.

Twenty years ago I wrote a book about IBM's internal culture[1], which seems to have changed remarkably little in the intervening period. One of the aspects of the company I still find most intriguing is the way IBMers feel such strong ownership of themselves and their own ideas, yet they also feel (or certainly used to feel) extraordinarily strong membership in the work group, the national company, and IBM itself. This empowering combination of ownership and membership merits close attention today, when so many other large organisations need to find ways to manage people through difficult times without disempowering them.

In profit or in loss, IBM is still demonstrably the world's leader in management and personnel policies, the company others try to emulate. That causes a problem for people (like me) who have for so long contended that treating people well is a major part of the recipe for success. IBM has actually capitalised on this reputation, turning it into a marketable corporate asset as IBM people begin consultancy assignments for other firms in quality, employee relations, and how to achieve excellence.

Cultural differences between UK and US observers have masked some startling changes in processes, practices and planning, all aimed at maintaining the *status quo* in how IBM treats its people. I see face-to-face communications, buttressed by the brilliant use of electronic communications, as the 'extra something' that helped enable the company to cope with difficult times. I also suspect that the very competence of that internal communication encouraged the 'smug factor', thus contributing to IBM's imperviousness to serious messages from the marketplace.

The Market as Framework

IBM's market-place has been changing. IBM's market was always the big mainframe computer, sold to corporate customers rather like IBM itself. IBM's 'OP' (Office Products) people, who sold typewriters to smaller firms, were always 'below the salt' and felt that their inputs were not taken very seriously.

Today the mainframe is a shrinking portion of the computer industry, and one even the Japanese are beginning to penetrate. The OP people who enabled IBM to enter the personal computer market never brought themselves and their messages to the top of the table. IBM stoutly claimed it must continue to cover every aspect of the computer market, to give full service to its big corporate customers. The competitors and *The Economist* believed otherwise[2]:

> No company, including Japan's Fujitsu, Hitachi and NEC, tries to compete in every segment of this vast industry – except IBM. Every other firm concentrates on where it can be best. Intel, Compaq, Apple, Sun Microsystems and Microsoft have all thrived this past year, despite brutal price wars. Companies with broader product lines based on large machines, such as DEC, Bull, Siemens-Nixdorf and Japan's computer makers, have seen their profits collapse. Like IBM, all are struggling.

Customers are changing too. Mainframes were bought by data processing managers in the olden days; IBM could call the tunes and set the standards. That is no longer true. When the customers are in the boardroom, IBM still knows how to win, though it can no longer count on fear or brand loyalty – just applications know-how. But when the customers are out on the street, or running specialist companies, IBM has a lot to learn.

Share prices started dropping in the late 1980s, and IBM had to do something. Chairman John Akers stated the situation rather blandly in the 1989 annual report: 'Rapid changes in technology and advances in manufacturing productivity have created over-capacity in both physical and human resources. Intense competition is increasing pressure on prices, margins and profitability.'

IBM tried to respond on four fronts: (1) more revenue from software and services; (2) better products; (3) lower costs; (4)

more IBMers close to the customer; (5) fewer IBMers. Akers tried to shift the development activities from technology-driven towards market-driven, and shifted people from overhead to customer-facing, but it takes a long time for changes like that to take root. In this fashion IBM became a pioneer in what is now a major trend among large companies: delayering, downsizing and empowering.

Breaking the company into 13 relatively autonomous units was Akers's response to bring faster reaction to the market. But large reorganisations take a long time to embed themselves, and by the time the new 'companies' had a chance to try their wings, Akers had first taken a 40 per cent cut in his pay (based on performance) for 1991, and then resigned.

The Introvert/Extrovert Conundrum

Today, whether the computer is large or small, people are buying solutions to problems, for which the computer is but a tool. In a market-driven world the computer is just a piece of the machinery, the engine but not the car. The know-how about the problem is the key to the sale. IBM was unable to know everything about everything, much as it would have liked to, so it had to learn to co-operate. This meant

- Other People sell IBM product.
- IBM builds Other Peoples' equipment into its systems.
- Other People develop the software.
- Other People have the user know-how.
- Other People make the components and deliver them, on time.

IBM was not accustomed to depending on Other People.

I think the greatest change in IBM's culture came about as the PC grew out of the typewriter in the 1970s – when IBM, to achieve necessary volumes, had to use non-IBM (Intel) chips in its PCs and let non-IBM people sell them. Living without full control – that was new! I believe the company was so busy teaching its excellent ways to the non-IBM people that it may have missed opportunities to learn from them about the real markets.

Where is the line between pride and smugness? A smug person or organisation feels good; it does not have to learn much from outside. So the seeds of its own destruction germinate in the cosy hothouse. When people spend so much time seeing each other behave so well, they tend to become somewhat intolerant of others less perfect. In retrospect, one can wonder what would have happened if IBM managers had learned 20 years ago how to manage the 'smug factor', rather than having to learn today how to manage redundancies.

Today IBM has moved on, trying to cohabit with such bedfellows as software firms like Lotus or traditional competitor Apple, or investing in specialist 'business partners'. IBM learned to co-operate (at least a little), and even sold off a few businesses. Even so, the company continued to have an exceptionally coherent set of beliefs and behaviour patterns. Mergers and take-overs are not within IBM's experience; only the current sense of crisis could make them work in such a consistent, pervasive corporate culture.

The Technology as Driving Force

IBM's choices have been 'technology-driven' since its inception in 1914. In a world where few computer companies have been good computer users, IBM's increasing tendency to practise what it preached helped to maintain an advantage. And at least in dealings with big, IBM-like customers, this strategy paid off because IBM understood how big, IBM-like organisations work.

In the early 1980s, for example, IBM decided it needed to use its own systems better to cut administration costs and make optimum use of network and computer investments. The result was a system called PROFS (for PRofessional OFfice System), which gave every IBMer his measure of information – and, I believe, helped materially in preparing people for the current crises.

By 1986 100 per cent of IBM's employees had developed keyboard skills – about 18,000 people in the UK (about 14,000 now), 90,000 in Europe, and they aimed for all 383,000 worldwide (now less than 300,000).

The implications of a single interlinked system are enormous! The typical IBM employee tunes to his PROFS screen from his office, his home, from a phone box, even (in the case of Sir Tony Cleaver, IBM UK's chairman) from the cellphone in his car. From a single screen and keyboard the IBMer can:

- view electronic mail;
- answer personal messages from friends;
- check his other diary;
- arrange a meeting (local or even international);
- look at the cafeteria menu;
- find out about new strategy decisions;
- check the share price and dividend;
- scan 'The car park will be closed this weekend for resurfacing';
- receive the chief executive's New Year greeting;
- check on standards or policies;
- access or change address, fax and phone number lists;
- find guidelines for writing a business case for a pet project;
- read book reviews;
- enrol for in-house or outside courses;
- read daily press highlights;
- look at the general processes manual;
- read the personnel director's answer to a speak-up question;
- book hotels and flights for the next trip;
- read notes of the department meeting missed yesterday;
- check Business Conduct Guidelines;
- view managers' information letters;
- scan organisation directories;
- check the organisation database for a colleague's new position;
- make quick reference to Purchasing facilities;
- look at Personnel practices and policies;
- read security manuals;
- write memos and reports, and more.

This kind of rich diet can become addictive. An ex-IBMer on a British Rail sleeper recently said he could put his Visa card into a machine somewhere 35,000 feet up, and put his computer in-bleeper to the phone mouthpiece, and it would automatically dial up his E-mail and give him his messages. He was rather perturbed that his in-bleeper would not work on the train's radiophone.

At first the PROFS proponents assumed 80 per cent usage would be in-group communication. But as soon as connection was universal and easy, communication with people outside the immediate working group skyrocketed — and with it rose the benefits of the expensive system.

For most companies, starting an E-mail system is like developing a television service: until there are enough people out there turning on their sets, there is no impetus or money available to make good shows – and without good shows who wants to buy a television set? So status-symbol 'manager-only' E-mail systems are actually starved of the information that enriches IBM's kind of PROFS.

There is clear evidence that company success is closely related to the richness of its informal human communications links. IBM's internal networks were certainly an unwritten but real part of its winning culture. I was concerned that the growth of PROFS may have eroded the phoning, travelling and meeting that reinforces such human networks, but an IBM spokesman contended that PROFS was not used to replace human contacts. They said IBMers could actually use PROFS to send informal message more easily, and they still had plenty of training, refreshers, and travel.

Chief among the benefits is faster decisions, a necessity in a company as huge as IBM. A PROFS expert told a professional group recently: 'If your information quality is good, then if you can speed up the information flow, you can speed up the decision cycles in the company.'

PROFS had to take some of the credit (or blame) for IBM's ability to recycle its people. IBM took the benefit of the PROFS-improved productivity by changing the jobs people did, and putting them into the revenue-earning areas of the company. More than half were in sales offices by 1991.

IBM insiders paid less for their equipment than customers who were sold new computers, but the insiders depended on older machines – proving once again that it is the management and training, not the technology, that makes the difference between a winning system and a white elephant. The annual cost per employee for PROFS in the UK has been about £700–800, including the network, technical support, depreciation, software, and so on. That is less than the UK company subsidy for the cafeteria in its Portsmouth North Harbour headquarters.

Personnel Policies as Backbone

Yes, the boss *does* eat in the canteen, at Portsmouth, at Greenock and at Armonk, and that has not changed in the past 20–30 years. The single-status cafeteria is one good example of IBM's sturdy, coherent personnel policies. Most other aspects of personnel management are single-status, too, although IBM UK managers do get company cars (they don't in the USA).

A strong, coherent and well-administered personnel strategy is, I believe, IBM's secret of success. How it endures under the severe stress of compulsory redundancy remains to be seen.

Respectability, one of the strongest threads in the fabric of IBM's culture, comes from its founder, Thomas J Watson Senior. In 1914 Watson (at the time under threat of going to gaol for sharp competitive behaviour at NCR, his previous employer) took over a cluster of little companies that made things like office clocks. Watson was determined that his company, rather optimistically named 'International Business Machines', would be the most respectable, worthy, and successful company in the world. He more or less succeeded. In days when salesmen wore flash suits and spats, IBM people were directed to dress soberly, eschew strong drink, and go to church.

Front-line Manager

Then, as now, the key person was what IBM calls the 'first-line manager', the one who supervises the 8–10 people in a basic working group. Since Watson first took over, IBM has always done everything it could to enable, empower and ennoble this basic manager. He (often she) hires, fires, decides the pay, and is the company's key communicator for his band of IBMers. And those well-selected, well-trained, well-appraised, well-counselled, well-surveyed, people are also well motivated – indeed, empowered. They always have been.

Open Door

At the same time, old Watson understood that differences would arise between managers and managed, and a disaffected employee could do the company's image harm in the small-town American environment of upstate New York. So he proclaimed: 'My door is always open'. And it was. That is the basic difference between IBM and other companies – it still is. In any Open Door disagreement, the employee receives the benefit of any doubt unless the manager has impeccable documentation to the contrary.

In practice, the employee goes to the level he feels is appropriate – frequently just to his manager's manager. He can nevertheless go to any other level, until he feels justice has been done. In a year the chairman's office might deal with two or three Open Doors regarding dismissal, a few more about advancement, pay, or being moved, some where the employee and his manager could not get along, and a handful of others. As troubles impended, the number of Open Door cases rose, from 16 in 1990 to 37 in 1991, for a population of over 15,000 in Britain – a useful investment in making sure that justice is seen to be done.

This was Watson's first known attempt to short-circuit the information filters that build up as organisations grow. Like members of Britain's Royal Family, he valued every opportunity to cut through ritual and to listen to his people tell it like it was. Open Door was inevitably ritualised somewhat, but it continued. Other forms of two-way communication also evolved, each with the same purpose – to keep the top in touch with the bottom.

Speak-up

This enquiry system gave employees absolute anonymity, so anyone with a question could obtain an answer, either in public through the company newspapers, or privately through the trusted senior co-ordinator. In 1991 the co-ordinator received almost a thousand letters, of which 127 demanded further management action. Most of the Speak-ups concerned pay, company cars, benefits, or office and administration procedures.

Performance Focus

Twenty years ago I wrote: 'IBM is a strict parent (especially for managers) but a good provider. The policy with respect to pay was and is to be about 7 per cent above the national norm (as IBM determines the norm among companies it considers comparable).' That has not changed at all. They call it Pay for Performance, and it is still the first-line manager who decides who is performing.

Pay for Performance

The direction is changing from worldwide norms to more local norms, and some IBM staff are concerned that their pay may not stay in the same range. John Akers wrote in the January 1992 annual report:

> Underpinning our efforts in 1992 is the continuing dedication of skilled and empowered IBM employees. Increasingly, they will be motivated by compensation more directly linked to the performance of the specific company, subsidiary, or business in which they work.

When a shareholder in 1992 asked how IBM would keep the best employees as it slimmed down, Akers went on to say:

> To retain the best people, we are emphasizing better rewards for higher contributors. On a broader scale, we are focusing more on performance planning, counselling, and employee evaluations, and we've raised performance requirements for all our employees worldwide.

Over the previous few years the definition of 'full employment' had already made a subtle shift towards more emphasis on the individual's 'choice', including choice to leave. Now the company was adding a sharper performance yardstick (and carrot).

The empowered front-line manager is the essential link in most of IBM's personnel policies; the fundamentals have not changed. IBM's basic values, stated by Tom Watson Jr in 1957, are (1) respect for the individual, and (2) pursuit of excellence.

'Respect for the individual' still drives personnel policies, but its manifestations move with the times. This codification of the Watson (old and young) principle is at the root of the empowered IBMer. Thus Pay for Performance carries a demand to give people the skills and tools to improve their performance. From this, in the 1960s and 1970s, IBM developed individual appraisal and counselling (A&C), which eventually evolved into one of the more open processes in large companies.

Appraisal and Counselling

This improvement in A&C is one discernible change for the better. A few IBM Personnel people used to hope it would become more helpful 'C', less gimlet-eyed 'A'. Today, it seems to me that they have achieved this.

Anyone doing less than well will hear about it long before the annual A&C session. To shift the emphasis, IBM has systems that literally force the manager to move around the table during the A&C session to sit with the employee and scan the organisation for individual development opportunities. This includes an Employee Development Plan, even an Employee Preparation Form, all with sign-offs and higher management reviews and follow-ups.

'It really is more open,' an IBM Personnel man says. 'The employee development side has more focus and emphasis now.' The IBM employee receives at least five days training every year. He or she is expected (and expects) to drive his or her own development plan. If the manager signs off the employee's plan as reasonable, then it follows that the manager has to help make it come true. The manager, in turn, is appraised from above and woe betide him if he or she has given his or her subordinate only lip-service!

Equal Opportunities

Respect for the individual implies equal opportunity for women and minorities, and IBM has set some good examples. Twenty years ago they appointed Patricia Roberts Harris, a black woman lawyer, to the main board. There are occasional unconscious barriers, as in many high-tech organisations. In October 1991 the company joined Opportunity 2000, and committed itself to have at least one female director on the UK board by 1995. The latest improvements have been in maternity leave and part-time or full-time return inducements.

Employee Surveys

IBM's famous opinion survey is alive and well, running every second year, as it has for more than 20 years. The content changes with time, but there are some core questions, so that they can track trends. In essence, the survey asks IBMers:

- What do you think of IBM?
- What do you think of your manager?
- What do you think of our personnel policies and how they work?
- What do you think of training, education, development?
- Salary and rewards?
- Recognition?
- Employee communications?

These are *all* things the company has demonstrated it will change if the employees are not content with them. Very few organisations are entitled to ask such question, in my view, without that kind of commitment. Some questions in the past, for example, concerned smoking. As a result of employee opinions, IBM changed its policy, and now British IBMers smoke in designated areas only.

For the past four years the opinion survey has been on-line on PROFS, and employees can E-mail the results back. The system was carefully designed for confidentiality, and everyone has a separate ID for the survey. 'You *cannot* trace a reply to an individual,' according to one expert. The response is encrypted as it is sent, and responses come back faster than pre-PROFS. 'We get flash reports more quickly now.' When the opinion survey asked employees whether they preferred it on paper or on PROFS, 95 per cent chose on-screen.

IBM have been aiming for 100 per cent participation in the survey, but used to get a little over 90 per cent. Since it went on PROFs the response rate is over 98 per cent. Easier access is probably the reason, especially for travelling IBMers.

Recognition

IBM's recognition budget has changed with the times. Each first-line manager has direct authority to give anyone in his group a recognition award. Originally this was in whatever form the manager thought best, flowers for the wife, gold pen with motto, and the like. Over the years it settled down to the equivalent of 'dinner for two', thus about £60. Even recognition can be ritualised. The employee is now given a form signed by his manager, which he then takes to the bank where he is paid the money, to spend as he chooses.

The place is peppered with awards and mottos, an approach to life that dates back to the elder Watson, but would be recognised by any Japanese factory manager. In 1991 1176 UK people won awards for 'Special Contribution', 'Exceptional Achievement', 'Outstanding Achievement', and 'Outstanding Innovation'. One manager has a fairly typical wall: seven awards or competence certificates and two fulsome farewell presentations.

Employee Communication

Employee communication has always been one of IBM's strong suits, based on regular team meetings conducted by the well-trained first-line manager with his team. The manager receives support in a number of ways. At Greenock, for example, with about 2200 employees, IBM had at least six people concerned with employee communications. As the economic situation worsened the company actually *increased* the number of employee communication specialists. The internal experts helped managers watch over a multitude of well-managed channels:

- UK and site meetings;
- Functional and middle-management meetings;
- First of the year meetings;
- Directors' communication meetings;
- Department meetings;
- Appraisals;
- Round tables;
- Leapfrog meetings and lunches;
- Notice-boards;

- Electronic mail;
- In-house publications;
- Speak-ups;
- Open door;
- Videos;
- Speeches and presentations;
- Communication surveys, and many more.

Noticeboards and Posters

IBM's noticeboards are always stylish. Greenock's are among the most handsome, each one 'owned' (some by veritable dragons who guard them watchfully). Every notice is up to date, attractive, perfectly aligned on the purpose-built sticky surface.

Greenock's reception has, in large brass letters, the same motto that adorned the key IBM building in New York City in the 1930s: 'World Peace Through World Trade'. In the halls you find a plethora of posters: 'Our Quality is in Our Hands', 'Quality *is* Our Business'.

The Personnel Function

Personnel, the core of the IBM culture, is running lean as the company tries to become smaller and fitter. Personnel used to be cells of specialists, in education, administration, communication, and so on. In 1988 they went through a 'cultural revolution' like Mao's: Personnel *apparatchiks* were sent out into the field to become generalists. They say the standards remained high, but the sense of utter control they used to emanate seems marginally lighter.

IBM has virtually no unions, except in those few countries where every organisation is 100 per cent unionised. In a 1977 ACAS survey at IBM Greenock, 94 per cent of the employees voted against union representation.

One manager with experience in the Clydeside shipyards just down the road from Greenock told me: 'We're union free because people trust the managers. They have good careers, and they feel treated fairly.' A 1988 survey by Tony Dickson and others at Glasgow Polytechnic and Strathclyde University found that IBM employees had no aversion to unions – they just felt they had no need of them. The well-trained accessibility of their first-line managers was an important factor in maintaining positive and empowered attitudes.

The 'Full-employment' Policy in the Mid-1990s

The 'full employment policy' was a cornerstone of IBM's culture. John Akers wrote in the 1990 annual report: 'We believe that the returns – in the loyalty, flexibility and productivity of IBM employees – continue to be a competitive advantage for the company.' At the same time he noted that IBM would do whatever it had to do to survive.

IBM's justification for full employment may have shifted slightly, from 'belief' to 'competitive advantage', but the cornerstone continued to stand until December 1992, when Akers had to warn employees that full-employment would disappear in some units – and he also told shareholders that their dividends would drop.

If you try to maintain a full employment policy you have to do your manpower planning with great skill. The company's internal planning has been extremely good but, like the rest of the company, the manpower planners had not quite anticipated how steep the 1991–2 drop would be.

IBM went through a tough patch in the early 1970s (when an 'Open Window' encouraged early retirement at 55). 'Full employment' might mean only one alternative job assignment, and that one in Denver, but stoic IBMers went where they were sent, and did what was needed.

The world-wide population of IBM employees dropped from 407,000 in 1985 to 383,000 in early 1990, and to about 300,000 in early 1993. Arrival of the new Chief Executive at Armonk heralded sharper cuts. The process might have been even more dramatic but for IBM's long-term manpower planning, and some lessons learned from experience, such as how to use the short-term and part-time cushions.

The economic crisis put a stop to IBM's aim to keep new blood flowing in. In 1991 the entire UK company hired only 11 new people, while the 'Career Transition Programme' helped several thousand leave gracefully. Fast growth in the 1960s gave the company an 'age-bump' that was already a visible problem, with about a third of the IBM population in Britain aged between 40 and 50, and a steady rise in the average age in this 'young men's business' to about 38 in 1989 and over 39 in 1991.

Outsiders In

IBM was one of the first to develop the idea of 'core' employees, though this concept is not stated as a policy. A few years ago one could begin to glimpse a series of 'cushions' as IBM began to bring in more consultants, more temporary staff, more part-timers, more student projects. Even in the stresses of 1991, when only 11 people were hired, 726 had student jobs in IBM and there were 225 YTS (Youth Training Scheme) trainees.

IBM did not want to stop recruiting, but the intake had to virtually stop in 1992. Those few who did come in were not always hired into a 'job for life' (or 'as long as he wishes'). In recent years IBM introduced four-year 'term contracts' for some graduate entrants, rather like a commission in the services, to give training and work experience to people who would expect to move on at the end. (Presumably IBM, like the services, could make new offers to those it particularly wanted to keep).

Another cushion came in part-time workers (about 400 in 1989), at least half of them women who were coming back part-time from a career-break scheme. Their numbers dropped.

The company made it quite clear that giving younger people career opportunities meant moving older employees down the status ladder. This was not so blatant 20 years ago, but many managers even then said they were 'looking downhill' from their 40s on.

Insiders Out

At the same time, more IBMers were encouraged to look at the outside via secondments or community links. Both were managed well. High-flying staff were sent out in the 1970s on secondments, then seen to come back into promotions. At a time when managers in other companies worried about being 'out of sight, out of mind', the IBMer had his Career Manager to keep him in view.

IBM, like Xerox and a few others, encouraged any employee to spend up to 10 per cent of his time on community activities of his choice. This was and is a strong motivator for most staff, though no one ever discerned the workload being reduced by 10 per cent as a result.

How did IBM slim down? Attrition was normally low, so they introduced large-scale attrition-encouraging programmess. [One new acronym picked up by an alert computer journalist was 'MIA', for 'Management Initiated Attrition' – otherwise known as 'Zap, you're dead!']

Special offers were made as inducements for those who wished to depart. In 1986 the company announced a voluntary retire-ment incentive ('VRI' in their parlance). A progression of inducements have been on offer since then, each with its own name (such as 'Career Transition Program'). Every country and every sub-unit has been given slenderising targets, and met them.

In the late 1980s VRI started at 53, but there were few takers at that age. More recently IBM sweetened the pot for a much wider range of employees, of virtually any age, who would like to leave.

Then IBM trained everyone left in the office, and moved many out into the front lines. The IBMers who remained were not making as much fuss as the outsiders looking in however; many were enjoying new challenges, finding new career opportunities. Certainly, they were more accustomed to moving. 'IBM stands for "I've Been Moved",' was one of my chapter headings in the early 1970s. (That has now gained a more recent gloss: 'IBM stands for "In Between Marriages," says one veteran. Divorce was rare in IBM in the 1970s.)

American employees have always been more willing than Europeans to move a few thousand miles to follow a job, or take a better one. Even so, employee mobility is diminishing, world-wide, as people realise that their loyalty to an employer is not always a guarantee of job security, and quality of life takes a higher focus for many.

IBM has certainly encountered 'sticky' situations, where the individual chooses to stay put because of his wife's job or the children's school. However, the corporate culture, and the practices that back it up, have at least three features that encourage mobility:

- The prevalence of assignments for development, coupled with the belief that being moved is A Good Thing, a reward for virtue.
- Everyone who goes on assignment has a Career Manager, someone back at home base chartered to keep the assignee informed, happy, and connected to the system – and to make sure that he or she comes back to a suitable job.
- Most IBM cluster sites have someone local who helps families settle in, arrange for the gas to be connected and the phone installed, not to mention introducing the family to the local social activities among IBMers and their neighbours.

Then there is the half-way house. IBM might not like the idea, but the exit-consultancy idea was actually pioneered about a decade ago by NatWest, and Rank-Xerox had its own form of 'in-house out-house' consultancy. Skillbase in the UK is 40 per cent owned by IBM; it offered the venturesome IBM employee with useful skills less certain but interesting opportunities for at least part-time consultancy in the outside world, with some short-term guarantees of work in IBM. This has tended to be for most a one-off one-year buffer rather than a new job.

New Models for Education and Training

Moving is development in IBM, and the depth of well-developed IBM people has demonstrated itself in the company's extra-ordinary ability to place so many thousand people into new jobs, even in new places.

IBM never did and probably never will do anything without proper training, planned in from the beginning. This is part of the problem of slow response times, but also helps to explain the wholeheartedness once movement begins. 'Training is always crucial,' says a manager, 'more than ever now. It's one of our key strategies to make sure we're competitive in education and training.'

One of the best examples is the Scottish plant at Greenock. The company has spent over £4 million since 1987 on education and training, including 'the University at Spango Valley'. John

McClelland, Greenock's former manager, is credited with this initiative. Needing a flexible, well-educated workforce, he looked at the Japanese educational profile. Japan has 55 per cent graduates, against IBM's 30 per cent, so McClelland developed a plan to take Greenock to a level similar to the Japanese by 1994 – by encouraging his employees to go to university on site.

IBM identified areas where it would need expertise, then set up agreements with Strathclyde University for management skills, Napier Polytechnic (now Napier University) for plastic skills, Paisley College of Technology (now the University of Paisley) for materials skills, and so on. The resulting 'university' had several significant features:

1. The academics send lecturers to the plant one afternoon a week to teach. Thus there is no travel, and there are no fees, for students because IBM pays.
2. There are no prior educational requirements – it is all open entry.

The company convinced the academics that 'equivalent professional experience' with IBM could be equal to a first degree. The first graduates in 1991 earned such qualifications as

- MBA
- MSc in Computer-integrated Manufacturing
- Msc in Plastic Moulding Technology
- HNC in Manufacturing
- HND in Materials Sciences

The last three did not even exist until IBM needed them.

Difficult organisational changes often look easy when IBM does them. In *Management and Machiavelli*[3] Tony Jay identified IBM's 'ten-man hunting band' as a basic element of its strength. That hunting band had weekly meetings, a well-trained manager, and clear objectives, so it was easy to turn it into a Quality Circle in 1980. From there it evolved into Total Quality Management around 1985, and to Just-in-Time manufacturing in the later 1980s. Each shift required great energy, but (compared with strenuous but not always effective exertions in other large organisations) all were virtually natural developments of existing momentum.

IBM has trained-in a succession of concepts over the years: decision-making, then situational leadership, and then contingency theory. That approach enabled IBM's rapid assimilation of quality ideas. The Peters and Waterman 'Managing Excellence' programmes were probably based on observations of IBM itself to a considerable (if unacknowledged) extent. 'Management Development and Quality joined forces and achieved real fusion,' a manager commented. Thus IBM could move on to running 'Quality as a Business', and more recently 'Post Zero Defects', 'Management of Change', and then 'Market Driven Quality' (with 'MDQ' posters on every noticeboard).

Every manager receives at least five days' training a year about managing people, in addition to the five days a year basic training for every IBMer. Unlike most companies, therefore, IBM can guarantee that a new concept is going to reach the entire management population within a year – and staff are sufficiently motivated to want to catch up if they hear that there is something new coming.

Management development is institutionalised, and is seen as an important part of the business. At the same time, 'respect for the individual', has been re-examined, and directed back on the manager's role in developing trust, justice, and *helping employees to take ownership of their jobs*. The empowered front-line manager is the basis for empowering employees.

A significant element of training since 1991 has been empowering itself, by that very name. In other contexts I am rather dismissive about 'sheep-dip training', but not so in IBM, where the machinery to follow through is so well honed.

Groups of IBM employees take part in 'empowering workshops', where they spend at least half the time deciding what they need to empower themselves. The 'teachers' become brokers to some extent, inviting in the targeted managers at other levels and in other functions, then helping the employees negotiate with the managers more effective ways of doing their jobs. 'Unlike most of our programmes, this one could be run by the employees themselves,' said one of the trainers.

In most companies pushing an idea like 'empowering' down into the workforce like this, over the heads of management, would be an invitation to disaster, but IBM employees, already relatively empowered in the midst of their uncertainty, are eager for more. Inside IBM in the mid-1990s, empowerment may just be the fulcrum necessary to pull the various strands of excellence together and to start building new momentum.

Notes

1. Nancy Foy (1973), *The Sun Never Sets on IBM*, New York: Morrow (UK title, *The IBM World*, London: Eyre Methuen).

2. 'To save Big Blue', *The Economist*, 16 January 1993.

3. Tony Jay (1976), *Management and Machiavelli*, London: Hodder & Stoughton.

19

BT: Doing More with Less

Surveys have helped BT achieve dramatic improvement over the past seven years, not only in employee communication but also in management style. The company's developments in these areas also demonstrate the 'change from the middle' principle, where the centre's role was originally to help a thousand flowers bloom. As strategic principles developed, the focus could then shift over a few years towards consistency of approach and economies of scale.

My experience in a single 'district' of BTUK during this yeasty time was a small part of a series of stories in every element of the huge company. It is a mark of the growing openness of the culture that BT executives are willing to let various parts of their story be published.

Background

In the 1970s today's 'BT' was the telephone and telecommunications portion of the ponderous Post Office, with all the heavy administrative systems – and excellent internal development – that went with stable civil service organisations in Britain. (In the

USA the term 'civil servant' is still a pejorative).

Gradually, over a few years, the Post Office sampled 'Industrial Democracy' (with workers on the board), then split into separate posts and telecommunications organisations. The new 'British Telecom' then experienced first the 'liberalisation' of its formerly captive market, then the highly publicised and over-subscribed 'privatisation'. In 1985 it reorganised itself from about 60 quite dependent 'areas' into 28 relatively autonomous 'districts'.

The march of technology was becoming a major issue as the UK's largest company invested billions in modernising mechanical telephone exchanges, putting high-capacity optical fibres into the ground in place of limited and expensive copper wires, and creating Europe's largest computer system to pull together all the information necessary to service 20 million households.

Taking BT's people along with all this change began to loom as a potential problem. Like people in many public service organisations, employees were conditioned to stable job-for-life ways, in an organisation where the rate of change was beginning to accelerate.

I first became involved in the company's activities in 1986, when Mike Bett (later BT's Deputy Chairman) was heading BTUK, BT's largest operating division, with about 90 per cent of its people. He set up a unit to specialise in employee communications; before 1986 the 'messages' had been the concern of Personnel people, and the 'media' (an august cluster of magazines and professional papers) belonged to Marketing, a situation found in many large organisations.

The First Great Survey: 1986

To help BTUK take a quick look at what other leading firms were doing, consultant Colin Minton drew together a cluster of communication specialists including Mike Arnott, John Raisin and me. After a few lively debates with the new in-house department and some discussions with sample groups of employees, BT devised a questionnaire to find out what its people thought of employee communications.

This 1986 employee survey was one of the largest ever conducted outside IBM. With over 200,000 employees, even a sampling approach meant 20,000 BTUK people receiving multi-page survey forms – even more than the 100 per cent IBM UK survey.

The BTUK survey came at an important time. Headquarters was becoming aware of the need for change, but it was a difficult period for technical people out in the districts. The company knew it had to change the age-old, inflexible rules and traditions about working, to be more responsive to customers, to bring in Total Quality Management. The worried engineers, and their union, were equally determined to resist change until the future was clearer. Morale was poor, and the press was beginning to enjoy picking on British Telecom for poor customer service, badly maintained phone kiosks, and rising prices.

At the end of 1986 it became clear that arrangements for feeding back the survey were not as sophisticated as the survey itself. The feedback took the form of a 400-page A4 book of numbers, with each question analysed in depth – but very little interpretation of what it meant. The book would be sent to each District General Manager. At an emergency meeting the consultants were assigned to various parts of the country, and sent out to do what they could to help interpret the findings for district management teams. Some districts wanted special meetings, others preferred summary reports. My area included Scotland and South Wales. Each district was to develop its own remedies.

In January 1987, just as the results of the survey emerged from the Harris computers, the engineers surprised their management and went on strike – a noteworthy cultural event in the company's long history of decent labour relations.

District Findings

On the first day of the strike, I was scheduled to present the (pre-strike) survey results to the board members of the East of Scotland District (EoSD in the jargon). I thought it would be difficult, under the circumstances, to concentrate their attention on new information about their employees' perceptions.

I underestimated the district management team. Perhaps the concentration of the board members was sharper in the absence of everyday interruptions. They were mainly in their 30s and 40s, quite a lively group of managers, led by Bill Furness, a management psychologist who had come out of the personnel function. Clearly they wanted to do whatever was necessary to improve their people's perceptions of the company. I tried to summarise 400 pages of data:

- Credibility wasn't bad. Nationally and in the district, 39 per cent of BT respondents felt fully or fairly well informed, and in EoSD 58 per cent believed what they were told (*v*. 54 per cent nationally).
- Face-to-face sources of information were few. About 50 per cent said that their actual sources for district information included hearsay, grapevine and rumour, compared with 36 per cent for external press, 63 per cent for *Telecom Today*, and 21 per cent for team meetings (*v*. 39 per cent nationally).
- District information was lacking. Fewer than 30 per cent were clear about district objectives, and only 23 per cent felt that they received enough information on how the district was performing.
- People wanted to hear about decisions from their own management, not through the national press; among the preferred sources for district information were team meetings (61 per cent), first-line managers (61 per cent), and senior managers (40 per cent).
- About 60 per cent agreed with the statement: 'No time is allowed for regular team meetings.'
- The board members were surprised that they were perceived as relatively invisible (92 per cent saw them once a year or less). People also felt the company was too secretive.
- The 'me' issues were paramount. Employees felt that the most important information was pay and conditions (53 per cent) and future plans affecting the district (47 per cent), job vacancies, and job prospects (36 per cent each).
- They wanted more information on job prospects and district plans (78 per cent), training opportunities (75 per cent) and future plans affecting the work group (72 per cent) – a fairly normal set of concerns.

Questions about what customers want brought out some

interesting contrasts. The employees recognised as 'very important' the desire for courteous and helpful staff (92 per cent),
but the Superman image crept in with fast response to emer-
gencies (94 per cent), fast maintenance (93 per cent), efficient and
fast engineering work (91 per cent). Keeping to promised dates
scored 90 per cent (but only 48 per cent believed that the company
met them). Factors the customers themselves said they valued
came further down the priority list – matters like efficient
paperwork (60 per cent), fast refunds (55 per cent), management
available to customers (50 per cent), smart, well-groomed staff (38
per cent) or clean vehicles (15 per cent).

In essence, people felt things were getting better for BT
(customer service, sales, ability to compete), and worse for
themselves (job security, industrial relations, pay). On the other
hand, 32 per cent already felt informed and involved, and
another 40 per cent wanted more involvement.

Improving Edinburgh District Communications

The EoSD board asked me to help them develop some remedies
for the problems the survey revealed. Bill Furness asked me to
work one day a week with Mac Farquhar, a young manager with
high commitment and recent training in quality. Bill asked us to
concentrate first on the 400-man Business Systems department,
which was pioneering the challenging combination of sales,
installation and service that later became a standard BT model for
business customers.

It was an exciting time throughout the company. The will to
change was strong, but not yet directed through a single leading
edge. A consultant friend remarked that headquarters was going
through a phase of matrix management: 'And at every inter-
section, there's some enterprising soul pushing out a new culture
change programme.' They were nationally in the middle of
Customer Care training. Some districts were putting their
managers through a Dale Carnegie course. The huge CSS
computer system meant more training for the thousands of
employees who would be doing their jobs in utterly new ways.

Significant investment was being made in Total Quality Management, which was just being pushed out into the districts.

Mac and I met in an empty office on the sixth floor of BT's Edinburgh headquarters, the same day that a TQM consultant arrived to begin interviewing top managers. We pencilled a hasty sign for the door, 'Consultants' Room'; from that time on EoSD kept its change programmes better co-ordinated than most districts, simply because the consultants tended to tell each other what they were doing as they shuffled their flipcharts and OHP transparencies.

Many ex-civil service structures start with grade 5 at the bottom, and go up to grade 1 at the top (like eggs). but BT management grades in the field at that time were reversed, starting with 'level 1', the front-line supervisor, and ranging up to about 'level 5', the District General Manager (or 'DGM' – its an alphabet-soup culture). In a delayering exercise, BT recently streamlined these to 'tier 1' through to 'tier 4'.

Encouraged by Russell Lee, the (level 4) board member who led Business Systems, Mac and I interviewed every one of his half-dozen level 2 managers, about 30 level 1s, and a cross-section of employees, in a number of locations in Edinburgh and Dundee. Some managers had staff meetings; one had 'proper team briefings'; others were too busy to hold meetings; all of them swore they kept their people up to date, individually and in their teams. The managers felt that some of the national survey findings were probably not too representative of their own people, who were better informed than average: 'I talk to my people every day!'

The group in Dundee showed high cohesion among themselves, but felt cut off from the groups in Edinburgh, whom they were sure were better informed. Various Edinburgh groups felt equally out of touch. Some of those in the same building as their top team felt particularly remote.

We started to sit in on meetings, wherever we could beg an invitation, asking people what they wanted to hear about, and how they wanted to hear it. People's comments matched the survey quite well. The level 1 supervisors were particularly concerned: 'Nobody ever tells us anything.' The group that had regular team briefings actually felt least informed; it turned out their level 2 was still loyally, dutifully holding a meeting every

Monday morning – from 9.00 until at least 12.30! These meetings were rather rambling work review mixed up with formalistic top-down information, without discussion. Questions were not encouraged so in an information vacuum, the level 2 was unlikely to have answers for them.

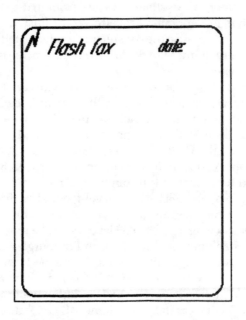

Figure 19.1 Flash Fax Form

A gregarious level 2 enjoyed a wide range of contacts around the company. His level 1s felt fairly well informed, mainly by dropping into the boss's office and chatting. His informal two-way communication was fairly good, but the troops who did not drop in felt just as left out of it as anyone else.

We reviewed our progress regularly with Russell Lee, who agreed that we needed a little 'system' to support the personalities. One of his people suggested a 'Flash Fax', so that every employee in Business Systems could see a one-page hand-written notice whenever something important occurred. This turned out to work well for them.

One acting level 2 was Ronnie Telford, an engineer and great-grand-nephew of the great Thomas Telford. Ronnie was about

47, a veteran of the Round Table and local rugby and golf club activities. His meetings were models of good communication: open, two-way, lasting about an hour once a fortnight. He did as well as one could in the absence of better information from above.

Ronnie began to take an interest in our project, and finally asked me quietly whether there was ever likely to be a full-time job in employee communications. We were just reaching the stage where Mac and I, part time, were feeling guilty because there was so much to do to support and coach the level 1s with their more regular meetings, though we actually needed to concentrate on improving the flow of district information and plans, and getting answers to the questions people were starting to ask in their meetings.

All the level 2s began holding regular meetings; The team briefer got his down to about two hours. Several began to spend more time out among their people.

Most of the level 1s also started to meet with their troops (though some only because they felt the pressure to do so). They still felt very exposed when people asked questions they could not answer. They said: 'Nobody ever tells us anything.' Their meetings tended to be stilted, one way. One said: 'You know, we've never had any experience at this. We aren't sure how to do it.'

Unanswerable Questions

Responding to questions was crucial – and we were the only 'machinery' to chase answers. In one of Ronnie's Sales groups, two level 1s had changed their people's schedules, with great effort and determination, so that they could hold regular fortnightly meetings and still keep the telephones covered. During their second meeting one woman asked: 'Dundee people have a discount at the telephone shop. I asked in the Edinburgh shop last week and they said we don't get discounts.' A simple question, and the leaders said they would check.

The query went to Ronnie the next day, but he did not know whether people were entitled or not. He sent it to Russell the following day; puzzled, Russell forwarded the query to Denis

Reay, the personnel manager. Denis made a few phone calls, but could get no answer to the simple-seeming question, so he forwarded the paper to headquarters, and continued to pursue it at least once a week.

Ten weeks passed – five fortnightly meetings for the Sales group, and with each meeting people grew more embarrassed as the leaders had to say: 'We still don't have an answer to your question about the staff discounts.' They could see their credibility dropping in the eyes of their people. It was Ronnie who finally heard about it again – he had naturally assumed they had already received direct answers.

In retrospect we can see what happened: telephone shops were new; there was literally no policy on staff discounts because no one had yet thought about the question. The Edinburgh query raised the question, and the policy-deciding machinery was taking its own ponderous time. In the meantime, Ronnie spoke to Russell, who spoke to Denis and Bill, and Bill announced firmly: 'Edinburgh people are to have the same discount in the telephone shops as the Dundee people.' Credibility was restored, at least locally – and we realised that if we were going to push the managers into having regular meetings, we owed it to them to invent machinery to help chase answers to questions from those meetings.

It was obvious what the 'machinery' should be, but inventing machinery takes a long time in large organisations. Ultimately Mac moved on to a job in Total Quality, and Ronnie Telford was transferred and became a full-time 'Combudsman' – a title we invented to take the job out of the normal grade-and-level thinking. As a level 1 'acting-up' to level 2 he would be working direct to 'the boss', Bill Furness (level 5), thus bypassing the natural ambivalence between Personnel and Marketing. This meant that Ronnie had to manage the relationships with those groups and their top managers like hedgehogs making love – very carefully. To increase their involvement and information, rather than leaving them feeling bypassed, he set up a co-ordinating group with Marketing and Personnel people.

Management Commitment

Employees, especially in Business Systems, perceived management's commitment to communication in a number of ways.

A Credible Manager

The appointment of a respected and credible front-line manager as Combudsman was viewed as a significant indication that Bill Furness and the district board really cared about improving employee communication in the district.

A Residential Workshop

Though budgets were tight and workloads high after the strike, Russell Lee agreed to pay for a 24-hour workshop for his 40 Business Systems managers, to review progress and have a first bite at training, now they knew that they wanted it. The 'District General Manager' Bill Furness, agreed to come to Pitlochry for the evening to keynote the meeting and obtain feedback from the level 1s. It worked. The managers recognised the commitment Bill and Russell were expressing.

Formal Communication Training

The syndicates and report-backs showed that many of the managers had never spoken in public before. They picked up a number of techniques and some practise, and asked for more training. Bill Furness agreed to divert a couple of good trainers to develop some two-day sessions for small groups of level 1s, with practice in front of a video.

Regular Meetings for Managers

As a result of the workshop feedback, Russell Lee agreed to hold a monthly 'Leepfrog' meeting with the level 1s, to try to update them on whatever was going on. Once the top and bottom managers were meeting, the ones in between began to feel pinched. They had to start feeding in more information themselves, even incomplete information, and they wanted to attend with their level 1s. The Leepfrog meetings were precursors for general management meetings that ultimately spread into every part of the district.

A Diary of Meetings

Russell asked for a diary of level 2 meetings, and then followed through by asking them to 'diarise' the meetings of their level 1s. Another powerful impetus against lip-service and for regular meetings was the story that spread around about how one level 2 had driven 30 miles to sit in on a level 1 meeting – which had been dutifully diarised – but not held.

The Mini-survey

When the Business Systems work had been under way for about six months and the workshop benefits were still fresh, Russell Lee wanted to check progress. He asked me to work with the 'team briefing' level 2 to distil the multi-page national survey form down to a single page.

I was rather dubious when the manager wanted to include tick boxes for the level 2 sub-units across the bottom of our survey form. He wanted to know how his own improvement efforts matched up to his brethren. The manager was equally dubious when I wanted to include space for write-in comments, to give us more reasons behind people's responses.

We discussed sampling, but actually decided to cover everyone, distributing forms through the face-to-face team meetings. The forms were to be sent back to me, outside the company, to ensure people confidentiality. Because they believed their results would be anonymous, and because managers explained the surveys clearly, 73 per cent of the staff returned them, which is a fabulous response in the survey business.

The forms gave us a rich source of candid information about the division. Some ignored the two-line space for 'Comments' altogether. Others wrote as if they were transcribing the Bible onto the head of a pin. Few could spell 'morale' correctly, but many mentioned it. Anonymous collections of the write-in comments went to the appropriate level 2 managers within the first fortnight. The managers seemed impressed at the quality of the ideas their people expressed – and concerned because so few of the write-ins were positive.

Because of the level 2 tick boxes, I was able to prepare separate reports for each of the six level 2 managers (with about 50–80 employees each). These showed the previous EoSD results, the Business Systems average for this survey, and their own depart-ment results on each of the 18 questions.

Next we met with Russell Lee's management team, giving them the report for the entire unit, and a league-table of results for each question. That is when I first began to respect the competitive glints in their eyes. Russell had anticipated this stage, and was enjoying the chance to harness his energy towards keeping people informed.

Finally, we took the reports right back down the line, giving each group a chance to discuss its own needs and concerns. Many of the issues from the national survey had boiled down to managers not communicating because they did not have the whole story, and employees assuming that being 'higher' meant being better informed. Employees at this stage all perceived some improvements from the national survey, even though the demoralising effects of the national strike were becoming evident everywhere.

Model for Improvement

Management was becoming more visible; meetings were happening, and more people found them useful – but we still had a long way to go. People were still as uncertain as before of what was expected of them, and few were getting the feedback they needed to know how well they were doing.

I have described the Business Systems pilot in some detail, because I think it contains most of the elements necessary to produce real, robust improvement in communications. General-ising from the particular:

- We had *top management commitment*, and found ways to show it. My presence as a consultant was often taken as a symbol of Bill's intention to improve communications.
- We were able to use the *national survey as a tin-opener*, to focus management attention on how their people viewed the communications.
- We *started where they were* – recognising and supporting good practise, while we encouraged the laggards to catch up.
- The front-line managers saw *enriched information*, changes that responded to their own requests: flash-fax and the Leepfrog meetings.
- Ultimately they received *answers to questions from the bottom*, and the district developed formal ways to follow these up.
- The *interactive training* was also seen as a result of their workshop.
- The 100 per cent mini-survey drew attention to their *progress* and the *internal league table* fuelled further improvements.
- The Appointment of the Combudsman meant that the *process was managed*. It was his job not only to chase answers but also to coach, encourage and nudge managers into keeping their people informed. He called it 'sheep-dog' monitoring – instead of the 'sheep-dip' inspirational training-for-all that characterises most corporate programmes.

Development in the District

Bill Furness and his board reviewed communication progress regularly, usually during their forward-looking meetings as the Quality Council. As TQM developed, we determined to avoid publicity for the communication work. Instead they treated it (like good training) as natural underpinning for other forms of culture change. In a period of many culture change programmes, this was useful for the district, and kept TQM as the leading edge for change.

I stayed closely involved in Business Systems until we were sure that the managers were taking responsibility themselves for pulling down whatever information their people needed. By this time Bill was informally moving the model out; other divisions were asking for mini-surveys of their own, and top managers were discussing and comparing how many of their level 2s held meetings. Several senior managers began MBSI, 'Management By Sitting In' on subordinates' meetings.

Everyone agreed that the lead division in MBSI and every other kind of employee communication was Finance, which included the large billing section and many of the new computer terminals. The Finance Manager was an attractive, soft-spoken, long-haired lady in her 30s named Joan Sweeney, whose people credited her personal drive and good example for most of the recent improvements. Meetings were regular and diarised; people understood what they were doing and why; senior managers were visible. Some other district board members were rather dismissive, however, suggesting that Finance was 'easy' compared with engineering management.

Competition is just as effective among senior managers as it is among front-line managers, and Bill Furness had a record of winkling out and developing good managers. He surprised everyone (including Joan) by appointing Joan Sweeney to run the largest group of field engineers – almost 1200 of them.

It should be noted that Joan Sweeney was not the only woman in BT who had reached the level of the district board. I believe it is BT's civil service history that helped give a number of able women a fairer chance to get past the first 'panes of glass' that sometimes hinder promotion.

Female and pretty doesn't mean soft or fuzzy; Joan was perhaps the most competitive member of the EoSD board. She buckled down to the engineering task with vigour, touring every location, asking people at every level what they had to do to win, asking her field-hardened managers difficult questions, personally attending every retiral or celebration. On snowy nights she was out with her emergency troops, and she expected her middle managers to be there too. She announced that she would attend team meetings of every group at least once a year; her subordinates were set similarly stringent targets for walking about and sitting in. Joan intended to run the engineering group the way she had run Finance, by making sure that people knew what was expected of them, and why, and how they were doing – and making sure they saw their managers. Regular and relevant meetings were an essential part of her style of management.

Ronnie and I helped Joan with surveys, feedback, improvement planning, and workshops for each group of field engineers. She, in turn, tied the league tables more closely to field performance than anyone had previously done, an approach which attracted close attention from her colleagues on the board.

In another division, a mini-survey revealed a serious hot-spot. The élite Technical Officers (known as 'TOs') were worried because they could see new technology replacing the mechanical exchanges they had for so long maintained. One by one the new exchanges were going in, but no information came down about plans for redeploying TOs. Their meetings (where there had been meetings) faltered and dried up as this most essential question went unanswered for another month, and another – the lack of response had gone on for more than a year.

We could not tackle their day-to-day communications improvement until the big 'me' question had some answers. Once Bill Furness saw how serious their situation was, he convened a special residential workshop; in a formal evening discussion followed by several hours informal chat, he told them there simply were no answers from elsewhere. The level 1 managers, hesitant at first, decided to take matters into their own hands and make interim plans for their people. They wanted to help as many as possible work themselves into new jobs gradually, but those remaining would have severe overloads. Bill, in turn, was able to find some temporary technical help for the overload period. Communication began to improve as the somewhat more empowered TOs and their managers felt less isolated. Ultimately, more than 200 were redeployed effectively.

Once again, we realised that *'conspiracy theory'* assumes that there are unpalatable truths out there, known to those higher up but kept secret from the troops. Instead, the typical large organisation problem stems from *'cockup theory'*, where no one has given a subject enough thought to have answers to communicate.

BT held another survey, piloting it in four districts in autumn 1987. EoSD was one of the select four. The results (rather dreadful overall, in the wake of the strike and press criticism) showed real EoSD progress in management credibility in Finance and Business Systems, as well as Operator Services which had well-established 'refresher' meetings. Bill began pushing harder for meeting diaries from every board member.

After the 1987 survey results came back, senior management credibility became an important issue in every district. Staff had reported back that they no longer believed to the same extent what their company told them.

The top EoSD managers saw that walking about and sitting in could not fill all the gaps, that their credibility depended on well-informed front-line managers. At the same time, people wanted more clarity about what was expected of their district. Bill Furness made a 'walkabout' video, discussing district objectives with local level 1s at Dundee and Forfar. This was used as the basis for discussions in team meetings. Joan Sweeney later made an award-winning video, discussing with some of her people how BT's 'massive' profits went into the huge investments in exchanges, optical cables, computer systems, and people. Ronnie Telford took part in making these videos.

Once it had someone to manage communication, the district was able to draw up *communication plans* and *monitoring* procedures, with the emphasis on managers walking the job.

National *survey feedback* was used as another form of monitoring, through the team meetings, with publication in the house newspaper and discussion at a new *management forum* for all managers, especially level 1s. The Combudsman monitored, in addition, with *face-to-face interviews* or *telephone questionnaires*, whenever he or one of the top managers saw a trouble spot.

Ronnie Telford had always been a well-regarded engineering manager. As his Combudsman role grew in credibility, my involvement diminished. By 1989 he was able to manage both national and local surveys from inside. He also played a pioneering role in developing a *network of communication managers* from northern districts. I was becoming 'emeritus' for the district, as a parent does when children grow up into worthy, responsible adults.

At Bill Furness's suggestion we started informal quarterly *one-day communication audits*, with three or four of us visiting sites, then reconvening with Bill at the end of the day to discuss progress or issues we had uncovered. These paper-free sessions gave Bill a chance to review forthcoming events that would need communicating, as well as current achievements and potential problem areas.

Progress continued steadily, through reorganisation and

changes of management. In October 1991 Joan Sweeney was accidentally killed by an electrical fault in her home. While the district and the company mourned, her people went on to demonstrate the kind of decent self-management she would have appreciated as a memorial. Her people played a major part in the sustained improvement in survey results. In the survey reported back in early 1990, twice as many of Joan's people perceived TQM as making the district 'better run'. Though job prospects for engineers were a worry throughout the country, Joan's engineers were still achieving the highest feedback on their own work group performance, as well as the highest scores on being able to speak up, and obtain answers to their questions.

The National Picture

One of BT's wisest steps in employee communication was the 1986 decision to let each key element and district find its own way to respond to the national survey. There was then no central machinery to monitor communication, and the survey itself was treated with a certain ambivalence for a time. Some districts brought in formal team briefing; some concentrated on improving house magazines. But once the questions were set by which they could be measured, the focus on face-to-face communication began to sharpen everywhere.

Just as competition was an effective spur to action among the level 2s in the district, and later among the district board members, so inter-district comparisons of employee communication joined the other indicators by which district boards were measured. A number of other districts fared better than EoSD in the early measurements.

The second survey revealed problems that management knew were lurking. The press had been involved in a virulent campaign making BT 'the company you love to hate'. These adverse comments reinforced staff worries and negative feelings, and the effects of the strike on morale and subsequent uncertainties about 'job repatterning' were visible in a number of ways.

- Fewer people were clear about their objectives and progress.
- Fewer people were proud of their work or felt a sense of achievement.
- Paperwork was seen to be rising.
- People felt less informed about the company, and fewer believed what they were told.

Team meeting scores as a source remained low. Information about job prospects had risen rapidly as 'most important' from 36 per cent to 66 per cent. Senior managers everywhere were seen (if at all) as weak or non-existent communicators, and viewed as uncaring, unreliable and untrustworthy. It was not a pretty picture and, a year on from the first expensive survey, it brought out adverse comment and close questioning from headquarters.

A close comparison between what people wanted to hear about and the topics discussed in their team meetings showed part of the problem. The supremely important 'me' questions were not being addressed. Here are the percentages of those saying that topics were raised rarely or never:

- pay and conditions   72%
- working hours   66%
- job prospects   65%
- people leaving/joining   64%
- health and safety   55%
- job repatterning   52%

The survey that revealed these problems also helped managers begin to cope with them, though not everyone appreciated that at the time. A combination of top-management commitment and expertise, and bottom-up monitoring, and management began to make the survey more of a strategic tool.

By 1988 BT deployed into employee communications Ruth Kirkman, trained and experienced in market research techniques, who moved from a marketing/product management job elsewhere in BT. In May 1989 John Steele became responsible for the total personnel function in BTUK, bringing experience of IBM's personnel philosophy and practices into the core of the giant telecommunications company. He knew from experience how useful employee surveys could be to concentrate management attention on employee perceptions. Steele and Kirkman's combination of commitment and expertise came at an auspicious time. Most districts had created employee communication managers by this time, and the surveys were increasingly being used to manage and monitor progress.

The BTUK board had taken an important step when it decided to tackle two problems that were harming the company's image. At a time when all other parts of the company were slimming, they hired extra people to help cope with payphone repair and maintenance, and cutting installation waiting lists. I believe that these decisions were an important turning-point towards empowerment for many BT people. As criticism receded a little, employees began to perceive that the company could, indeed, manage itself proactively and act decisively. They began to see that their supertanker could turn.

Ruth Kirkman managed the first quarterly tracking survey in late 1988, fed back in early 1989. I worked with her to pilot some new questions, and make sure that employees were comfortable with the new survey forms.

Credibility was up everywhere (from 43 per cent to 55 per cent of staff who always or usually believed what they were told about BT). In EoSD there was an amazing rise from 30 per cent to 61 per cent. The EoSD team meeting score was still below the national level, but it had climbed sharply from 19 per cent to 54 per cent! People still wanted more information than they were getting from line managers and senior managers.

Nationwide, 56 per cent agreed that 'BT seems to know where it's going' (up from 31 per cent the year before), and even the sense of achievement was creeping up, from 17 per cent to 28 per cent. Other aspects which were seen to be getting better (or less worse) included the public's attitude to BT staff, job security, stores availability, industrial relations – and employee communications.

Full-scale survey results were fed back in February 1990 in an excellent 24-page summary book for managers, with good graphs for each district and function. The early improvements and concentration on team meetings were beginning to show results across the country. Those who had meetings monthly or more frequently were finding them increasingly useful as a source of information. The continuing effort to ensure that questions were answered was also useful. Nationally, there was a problem area: in every district the operators, facing new 'handling time' demands, were having fewer meetings and feeling less informedddd..

Like the districts, BTUK itself evolved its employee communication strategy gradually, as more information came in about employee perceptions in headquarters and in districts. I am aware that other parts of the company were also evolving communication initiatives, but I have less information about their activities. With each survey, the focus sharpened. By 1989 district management teams knew that they were being judged on how well their people scored managers on walking about and sitting in. Inter-district league charts officially existed for survey scores, and the responses for 'informed' and 'believe' were at the top of them. The heat was on.

Postscript

The district organisation was changed dramatically in 1991, with the massive 'Sovereign' reorganisation, into two organisations relating respectively to business and residential customers, and a third managing the world-wide networks (an inadequate and early description of a massive shift in focus, towards the customer). The company (renamed 'BT', no longer 'British Telecom') also introduced a major programme to offer managers early retirement. Then, before the new organisation had really bedded down, came 'Release 92', with generous early departure terms for employees at any level.

The communication task was massive – and well managed. Every employee had an interview with the immediate boss, and a clear indication of what the terms would be if he or she left. Because the pot was sweetened considerably, a great many people asked to go, and then could not be released. This created feelings of discontent on occasion, but the company determinedly kept communication very open, publishing and discussing letters of complaint in the house journal *BT Today*, and frequently restating the reasons for the programme.

In an awesome demonstration of the efficacy of employee communication, nearly 20,000 BTUK people left the company on

31 July 1992, with hardly a mention in the press, and this in the year when a similar number of equally well-cushioned departures proposed in the coal industry had led to massive marches on the streets. The BT people who were given the Release 92 terms felt that they had some choice in the matter – though many of them also felt a tremendous wrench at leaving the organisation they had served for their entire working lives. Release 93 followed, and some employees were scheduling themselves for Release 94 and Release 95. The company continued to place a high value on voluntary departure.

Over the past few years BT has gradually redefined the word 'manager' to include someone who keeps his or her people informed, recognises their achievements, appraises them regularly, and earns their belief.

As many can attest, the focus on the customer has improved dramatically, with more than 95 per cent of payphones working, and most appointments scheduled at the customer's convenience. Many engineers have received extra training so that they can now show and provide new equipment when they visit a customer with a maintenance problem. Bureaucracy never disappears in large organisations, but it has visibly diminished in BT. In my view, BT's once staid culture really has changed.

Part IV

Resources for Empowering

Throughout this book I have referred to various communication channels, to survey elements, and to writers whose work provides a basis for empowering people at work. Part IV contains three sections for people who would like to explore further for themselves:

- *The A–Z of Communication*, an annotated alphabetical list of communication channels – an *aide mémoire* from which the user can put together an appropriate selection for a specific organisation.
- *The Pick and Mix Survey*, a selection of survey statements that can help an organisation ask people how they see themselves and their management.
- *Recommended Reading*, a list of some favourite management writers, generally those whose work has fed into today's empowerment models.

An A–Z of Communication

Developing a communication strategy can help a large organisation empower its people – by reducing the conflicting, misleading or delayed messages to ann absolute minimum, and making sure the listening channels are tended just as well as the telling channels. The most telling channels are those listening channels.

Working on the initial communication strategy, then reviewing it regularly in light of current experience, is a way of making sure each channel is properly maintained. Every channel needs:

- to be 'owned' (as near the ground as possible);
- to be monitored (as near the top as possible); and
- to be used with good sense so that it goes on carrying useful information.

Most of these descriptions assume you have (or plan to have) someone managing employee communication virtually full time in a large organisation. Some of the communication manager's duties can be part time in a smaller or simpler organisation, or one basking in steady-state euphoria. For most fast-changing modern organisations, however, an able, proactive, change-helping person should be available to manage and monitor communication.

I have listed the channels here in alphabetical order, so that you can find them easily. They are:

Annual report
Appraisal
Audit
Awards
Badges
Community evening
Customer complaints
Electronic mail
Employee handbook
Employee survey
Fax
Front-desk communication
Grapevine
Group meeting
Hot line
House journal
Informal networks
Informal social events
Joint council
Leapfrog lunch
Letters
Letters to the editor
Management audit
Management brief
Management by walking
  around (MBWA)
Management by sitting in
  (MBSI)
Management forum
Management letter
Mass meetings
Names
Network
Newsfax
Newsflash
Newsletter
Notice-board

Open day
Open door
Open staff evening
Organisation chart
Phones
Phone-in newsline
Photo organisation chart
Recognition
Roadshows
Royal progression
Safety representative
Speak-up
Staff meeting
Staff representative
Suggestion scheme
Tannoy system
Team briefing
Team meeting
Team meeting notes
Thank you
Training refresher
Video
Walkabout

Annual report This document, usually confined to share-holders, can be used to help employees see their efforts in context. It tells them how much they have produced, what income it has generated for the organisation and how that has been spent on tax, salaries, investment and dividends.

Some organisations produce a report especially for employees, which can also include indicators like safety, employee turnover, and absenteeism, or comparisons from one region or function to another. Numbers or graphs are not particularly interesting unless they ask and answer: 'why?' Are results good or bad? How do they relate to objectives for the next year?

Distribution and discussion complete the process. Share-holders receive their reports by post. Copies for employees should go by the same post. That is the most effective way to send out an employee report, too, unless it takes a tabloid form, as an insert to the house journal. (In truth, the house journal would be better read if it is posted to people's homes, too.) If team meetings leave room for discussion of team results in terms of the reported organisation results, you can increase the take-up and usefulness of the results.

Appraisal An increasingly important vehicle for one-to-one communication about people's performance, both their expect-ations and achievements. Top managers need to set the example as well as the requirement, by making sure that they do a good job of appraising their own subordinates before imposing an appraisal system across the board. Formal individual appraisal, usually an annual or semi-annual affair, needs to be matched by more frequent group mechanisms (for example, Performance Review as part of the agenda for normal team meetings) plus regular informal feedback (at least once a month, and when significant milestones occur) from one's own line manager. See Chapter 15.

Audit Feedback can help managers tell their people whether they are winning or losing, and reasons why. Some organisations have in-house consultants who audit various elements. In other places out-house consultants are brought in regularly, to monitor the organisation. One way is to send managers into less familiar parts of the organisation – a do-it-yourself approach. By trying to assess the success of other groups, and working together to do so, the organisation gains by a good audit, and development of the auditors. If DIY auditors have to feed back (and defend) their findings to all managers in the unit they audit, the learning is shared even more widely.

Awards Three years after Chris Greene left ScotRail the tea stall on Queen Street Station in Glasgow still sported a little plaque with his signature, commending it for cleanliness and cheerfulness. People appreciate thanks in any form; an award underscores what the organisation values, not only to someone who receives it, but to everyone else who sees the prize. See also 'Recognition' and 'Thank you'.

Badges In some organisations the wearing of a name badge denotes higher status. In others only the lowly are badged. Badges as hierarchy markers are disempowering. On the other hand, a badge with a person's full name on it, in large and legible type, can help communication immeasurably. See also 'Names'.

Community evening Most organisations leave their communications with the community in the hands of public relations people. Good neighbours can be invited in various ways to come in for coffee and chat with a cross-section of managers and employees. Communication is often best without too much one-way presentation.

Customer complaints These contain essential information to let people know how customers perceive their performance. Most organisations go to great lengths to keep complaints secret! If, instead, an organisation regularly publishes the number, categories, and solutions in the house journal or via management newsletters for group discussion, people can discern more clearly what they have to do to meet the needs of customers.

Electronic mail Some companies use systems such as Micro-Mail or PROFS for rapid transmission of news items as well as the whole gamut of business communication. Successful use of E-mail tends to depend on two factors: (1) the proportion of essential information that arrives electronically, and (2) the proportion of people in the organisation who use it. In other words, until your own boss and your own colleagues are sending you items you value, you will not use E-mail very often. Even in the best-run companies there is frequently resistance to the march of technology. Watch out for the top executive who only uses it through his secretary. One large company that restricted PROFS to managers only is still wondering why no one obtains full value from its sizeable investment.

Once you have good usage you can do things like employee surveys very easily. As Chapter 18 shows, the keys to E-mail success are

- terminals for all;
- keyboard training for all;
- informal, irreverent, interesting communications;
- personal privacy.

Employee handbook Everyone deserves to know the rules, and procedures that affect them. A short, plain-English employee handbook can help, with hours, entitlements, restrictions and dispute or grievance procedures. It should include pointers to the more formal documents where necessary, rather than trying to dot every i and cross every t.

Employee survey As Chapter 17 shows, regular employee attitude surveys can be used to monitor people's perceptions and concerns, as well as the progress of empowerment and change programmes. This cannot, however, be done in a vacuum. Someone has to 'own' the survey, feed back the data, and make sure people act on it. Anonymity is vitally important for employees. Short surveys can be particularly useful; survey 100 per cent of staff in a large department or function, with an indication of sub-groups where that does not endanger anonymity (usually for groups larger than 20). A trusted communication manager can feed back findings and help managers use them to plan the improvements that the staff want. Subsequent surveys should not be more often than annual.

Fax The machinery is widespread, yet not much used for employee communication. A communication manager may be able to help dispersed organisations use their fax facilities to good effect. Fax is ideal for transmitting press reports or clippings for notice-boards in every location. It also handles drawings, photos and charts well.

Front-desk communication Use the receptionist in each location or department as a focal point for employee communication. This front-desk communication centre might, for example, have a notice-board with Newsflashes (q.v.) showing current (today's) press releases and clippings. People appreciate hearing the latest information from a receptionist verbally.

Grapevine This is how most people gather most of their information in most organisations. They do not, however, *want* to hear it first on the grapevine; they want to hear it first from their own manager. The manager often hears it first from them, instead. Good communication does not have to drive out the grapevine, when the manager can beat the grapevine fairly regularly, and be more dependable everyone is more likely to feel empowered.

Group meeting Whatever you call it, the meeting of the basic work group is the most important communication channel of all. Without it, the rest is window-dressing. See 'Staff meeting', 'Team briefing' and 'Team meeting'. See also Chapter 14.

Hot-line Some companies use an answering machine to collect anonymous comments or questions, then feed back answers through the house journal. This approach can fill up with trivia if it is not monitored closely, owned, and personally administered by a senior manager. I prefer a less mechanistic approach that depends on the trust people have in the senior co-ordinator. See 'Speak-up'.

House journal Publishers put millions of pounds into public newspapers, yet the average top executive pays virtually no attention to his in-house paper. Thus its comparative ineffectiveness cannot be too surprising. People still see the house journal as the most important source for company information in many organisations. *What a waste!* Robert Benchley in 1922 considered that most house journals reveal more about the misconceptions of the management than the interests of the employees:

> Perhaps someone will start a house organ edited by the employees for circulation among the bosses, containing newsy notes about the owners' families, quotations from Karl Marx, and the results of the profit-sharing contest between the various mills of the district. This would complete the circle of understanding.

Few house journals have editorial involvement from the top. Lowly, lonely editors (often without professional training or editorial access) are left to wallow in trivia of their own devising. If they do try to publish interesting, relevant items like performance information, management often criticises them. Performance indicators can go down as well as up, but they have to be true to be worth asking people to identify with them.

A good house journal needs editorial policy, good distribution, feedback from the readership. The objectives of the house journal – to support the communication strategy – should be to help people feel involved and informed, in an organisation that accepts and relishes change. It should include information people have already heard from their managers, with more background and explanation.

On the less formal side, the house journal should also answer the question, 'who are we?' This calls for profiles, vignettes, sports, features about interesting people. These days another role of the house journal is to tell everyone about the good works the company and its employees are involved in, such as charities, the environment, and so on.

Informal networks Most organisations already have some lively informal networks, though some managers actually feel threatened when their people acquire information effectively through their personal sources. In a healthy organisation the formal and informal sources all work effectively, and reinforce each other. The trouble is that busy people often cut short the informal time they need to listen to each other without agendas and action items. More networks are needed in most organisations, crossing site and function boundaries – not so much for action as for sharing experience and informal information. Thus you need more meetings with coffee or a meal first, or an extended tea break, and more space in agendas for 'any other business', from the members, not the chair. Like any other communication channel, an informal network needs to be owned and maintained. Experience shows that a network needs:

- a permanent (stationary) point of contact;
- a list of members, with full names, jobs, phone and fax numbers;
- a diary of regular meetings.

See Chapter 12 for more about information networks and action networks.

Informal social events Many events stop when reporting lines change. In fast-changing organisations people need each other more, not less. In a reorganised unit try to identify the people who used to organise events, or else create a communication committee to create new events.

Joint council This can be an important and valuable means of listening to employees through their representatives. Like any other means of communication, such meetings improve with good, timely feedback.

Leapfrog lunch In some organisations senior managers try to meet regularly with groups of their subordinates, as another means of monitoring and managing. These can range from intimate small gatherings to perhaps a dozen from across the organisation to meet with the chief executive and hold an open discussion about issues of their choice; these meetings might be followed up by a note-taker, or even reported in detail in the house journal. That works best if the photos feature the employees rather than the chief executive.

Letters Letters and memos are often sent merely to confirm information. With workloads rising, work groups may want to start 'paper-chase' activities. *Letters are the least useful form of communication.* They usually keep people from doing real communicating.

Letters to the editor This is the exception that proves the letters rule. You can often judge the open culture of a company by the degree of criticism it permits in its house magazine. Letters that are critical of management are often over-edited, or are answered with too much self-justification. This can dry up the flow of good letters. If employees cannot discuss important matters in the company newspaper, they can always use the local newspaper. Managers in a company with an anodyne, soporific house journal are usually avid readers of the local newspaper.

Management audit A management audit might be done *by* managers, or *to* managers, or both. Feedback from audits can help managers tell their people whether they are winning or losing, and reasons why. Financial audit approaches could be extended to cover management aspects of effectiveness: co-ordination, communication, and especially performance reporting. See 'Audit'.

Management brief Many organisations use a formal paper or newsletter to keep managers informed of higher-level decisions, appointments, events, contracts, and so on. Ideally, the brief should be timely, relevant, short, and explain the reasons behind the items. Ideally, it should be issued at least once a month. Ideally, it should be open to the manager to decide how and what from the brief to tell his subordinates. *Ideally, the brief should not replace a proper team meeting structure.* The world is not always ideal.

Management by walking around (MBWA) This is one of the most
important forms of management communication, not only to make managers visible and accessible, but to force them to confront real information, as well as all the paper with which their desks become cluttered. Performance should be the focus for MBWA.

Management By Walking Around can be an embarrassing ritual, or it can be a senior manager's greatest source of information from the front line. Max Palevsky used to arrive at his computer company in California at 7.30 in the morning, and start walking around talking to whoever was in the offices or factory. This not only gave opportunities to people who wanted to talk to the boss about something, it also encouraged good time-keeping. Max's hands-on style entitled him to the $100 million or so he walked away with when Xerox bought out his company in 1969.

The manager who mixes with his people is better able to withstand the impenetrable 'felting' that befalls middle managers in large organisations where blame tends to be apportioned easily. It happens to the Royal family too; I recall a meeting of the Chartered Institute of Transport where Princess Anne kept the VIPs waiting for over an hour for their dinner while she asked each lowly member about his or her own job.

Management by sitting in (MBSI) Managing, monitoring, listening, and being visible simply by sitting in on the group meetings of subordinates. This demands a proper schedule so that the manager covers every group in his or her department, it also demands open eyes and ears, and a closed mouth.

MBSI is particularly effective for monitoring as well as listening. In BT senior managers are expected to sit in at least twice a year, and directors or board members at least once – a major commitment in time for the more senior members of staff. The senior managers have that target written into their objectives in the company's Performance Management System.

Management forum Here the top team tries to convene and communicate with all managers in an organisation at once. Its success as top-down communication may be limited, but it can be very useful to reinforce the management networks, if enough time is allowed for coffee and discussion or syndicate work. The mechanism can be useful for communicating a single important message – for example, the results of a large survey, or financial performance for the period. Its usefulness is directly related to the chance managers have to discuss among themselves and understand the information.

Management letter This is appropriate whenever there is something to say to a large number of people. A manager at any level can use this channel to reach all staff or all managers, though it tends to be used most by top executives. People will usually want to discuss issues in staff meetings after receiving a management letter about an important topic.

Mass meetings Commonly known as a 'conference'. The management mass meeting tends to be held in more comfortable surroundings than a union mass meeting. There is room for organisations to have more conferences for more groups of workers. How about the supervisors' conference? The cable jointers' conference? The bottling plant workers' conference?

Names People's names are important to them. Using them properly conveys respect for individuals, just as 'Mister' and 'Doctor' and 'Sister' do for senior health professionals, or 'Professor' and 'Dean' do for academics. But titles like these can sometimes be put aside to increase informal communication. The British habit of using initials rather than first names on badges and lists actually hampers people's ability to talk easily, informally, with others. Many people file by first name.

Newsfax An easily recognisable form to contain information of general interest could be used to fax news to notice-board owners or communication nodes in every relevant working area. Newsfax requires managing, and thus ownership, like any other channel. See 'Fax'.

Newsflash A one-page, hand-written form (similar to the meeting notes form) can help people at any level to capture information they feel is relevant to their colleagues or subordinates and post it in a central place. Content might be:

- a clipping;
- hand-written summary of a radio or TV item;
- copy of a photograph or cartoon;
- brief message faxed from top boss;
- thank-you from middle manager to specific group;
- local engagements, weddings, birth, social events, and the like.

Supervisors or notice-board owners in every area can distribute the forms and encourage people to use them. They only need to be posted for a day or so. The main screening would be of relevance to that group, determined by its own members and supervisors.

Newsletter People are most interested in their own departments, functions or work groups. Informal newsletters are usually believed and appreciated, regardless of spelling or production method. *Fastest is best*. Excessive professional polish at the local level actually detracts from credibility. See 'House journal'.

Noticeboard Noticeboards are widely used by most employees, but seldom by their managers – which explains why they often look so unmanaged. The noticeboard is more immediate and more important than the front page of the company newspaper. This is where the *urgent information* should go, not the fading, yellowing policies of yesteryear. Adair says that 'urgent' means 48 hours, no more.

Each noticeboard needs to be owned; it will then be possible to have a network of owners to develop and monitor 'rules' for content. Every notice should be owned, too, preferably with the owner's name and its sell-by date marked on it. You need a clear distinction between 'under glass' and 'open access' noticeboards. Most organisations have too few boards in places where people can stand around and read them, such as staff canteens, coffee areas, front desks, in or beside the lifts.

Open day An opportunity for employees or neighbours to come in and see the organisation. If employees of a group are able to put together informal demonstrations or displays the involvement can be high, and their amateur efforts are more likely to be credible (and generate enthusiasm) than elaborate shows from more remote experts. Food and fun for the children contribute to the success of such an event.

Open door A technique made famous by IBM, way beyond its linguistic origins ('My door is always open . . .'). In the IBM model any employee with a complaint is entitled to go to higher management at any level (usually the grandfather or great-grandfather, but occasionally the very top of the company – wherever he or she feels redress will be gained). It helps if the employee is assumed to be right unless proven otherwise; this means that any time a manager is going to do something that will probably upset an employee, the manager has to be sure that every i is dotted, every t crossed, and records kept to prove it.

This way, open door is a useful way to defuse grievances. It is not a bad way to keep managers aware of what upsets people, too. In many cases the result of an open door is that the manager and the employee have to be put in different parts of the company. It is a useful technique; without recourse or escape, the employee with a difficult boss is as much a hostage as a child with a cruel parent.

Open staff evening This could be held as often as once a quarter, with one or several top managers present. In very large organisations some employees never see 'the boss' in the flesh. Ideally the format is merely employees asking about things that concern them. As with any form of walkabout, the leaders can use a note-taker to record and follow up on queries.

Organisation chart The 'org chart' both describes hierarchy and reinforces it. It also tells people who is doing what to whom. The worst situation of all is the rigid hierarchy that keeps its org chart secret! Conspiracy theories and micro-politics thrive in such mushroom factories.

People want to know who their bosses are, and how they relate to each other. In places where good organisation charts are published, most employees post them on their office walls. See 'photo organisation chart'.

The boxes and lines of hierarchy on organisation charts are too limiting. I would like to see a world where each work group could clearly describe its own place in a network of circles, or hexagons, or even cloud shapes, with wider or narrower arrows of information flowing among them.

Phones Phones are used to make appointments, for quick contact, to obtain information. In a rapidly changing organisation, an effective phone book is essential, including an A–Z of all individuals, with their full names, locations, job titles, and how they can be reached by phone.

Phone-in news: The 'open line' or phone-in information can be useful if it is owned and updated well. It leaves the initiative in the hands of the listener – so the editor needs to feed the listener's interests. Phone-in can be useful for quick reporting of:

- this week's performance figures;
- construction or parking changes that will affect employees;
- today's canteen menu;
- today's share price;
- today's site visitors;
- today's newsclippings or press releases about the organisation;
- a one-minute explanation by the managing director of the poor quarterly report.

Like any other medium, phone-in needs to be 'me', local, relevant, and changing responsively. If in doubt, if it is not to be owned by an enthusiast with enough time to maintain it, don't start it!

I recall sitting in one district of a large company that used phone-in lines, and ringing five other districts. Two had information at least three months old; the others more than one month. I doubt if anybody else had phoned any of them. (This is the quintessential railway situation: 'Nobody's using this line, so we might as well axe it', rather than improving the frequency of service and making it do what it was designed to do.)

Photo organisation chart It helps to have people's names and faces posted, for local recognition, by insiders and outsiders. Each location can feature key people (including secretaries) on a photo chart. The top management chart can also be visible for staff as well as the public at main reception areas. It is particularly effective if a good photographer gets most people smiling in a friendly fashion. It is less effective if the chart cannot be changed unobtrusively when people change jobs. I do not know which gives a worse impression: the chart with a torn mystery gap, or the chart that includes faces everyone knows have been gone for months.

Recognition Some companies put power into the hands of front-line managers (that is to say, supervisors) by giving a certain sum of money (say £25 per employee in that group per year) for appropriate forms of recognition, immediately it is deserved. A £15 pen from your own boss the week you finished a project is more motivating than a pre-programmed rise of £1000 at the scheduled time for review. Similarly, a bunch of flowers to the wife of a man who worked all weekend, or an impromptu Chinese dinner for a late-working group can be important forms of recognition. And in some 'dry' companies the recognition budget is the only way a bottle of champagne can be funded to mark a group achievement. See 'Thank you' for even lower-cost forms of recognition. See also 'Awards'.

Roadshows Closely related to the mass meeting, the roadshow is a performance by the chief executive, or members of the top team, who go out to all locations within a short period to explain and discuss an issue. There are dangers when roadshows become too slick and one way. Ex-theatrical producers assure us that the roadshow is the new form of communicating with people, known as 'orienting their information and values'. Despite the propaganda danger, roadshows can be appropriate for large issues that affect everyone, where top management needs to be seen in person and to be seen listening to discussion. Everyone receives the same message. It can be exciting and fun, but watch out for hypocrisy perceptions, especially if the organisation is tightening its belt in other realms, or if it is the first communication people have been subjected to for several years.

Royal progression A polished performance, usually by a top-level executive. Though this is often one-way communication (downwards) and highly stage-managed, an adept leader can use the RP to give the personal touch, and an opportunity for inspection and inspiration.

Safety representative Walkabout is an important part of any safety programme. Safety Reps deserve respect and reinforcement when they observe improvements that would be useful. How hazard lists are dealt with affects the credibility not only of future hazard-hunting approaches but also of suggestion schemes and quality projects.

Speak-up A system for gathering concerns, queries and complaints from employees through a respected 'ombudsman'-type co-ordinator who maintains the anonymity of the employee and demands answers (preferably platitude-free answers) from senior managers. These can be published or fed back privately, as the anonymous employee prefers. Chrysler and IBM are among the companies that use speak-up well. In most organisations only about 30–40 per cent say 'yes' if you ask whether it is safe to say what you think. Managers are often more afraid than shopfloor people, who have elected representatives and other mechanisms for speaking up. The questions people ask in a speak-up programme range from personal niggles to important issues. They have to be handled openly, yet with personal anonymity. No matter how good the ombudsman, the scheme will fail if the responses contain waffle. See 'Hot line'.

Staff meeting Yet another name for the one where we talk about matters that are important to us – our work. See 'Team meeting'.

Staff representative Reps have a broad role to represent the views and needs of their members to management in a negotiation setting. If managers do not involve staff Reps in the communication process, the organisation will suffer by less effective negotiations.

Suggestion scheme Staff don't demand high monetary reward for making suggestions for improvement, but they do need rapid and positive feedback when they make suggestions. Many firms present an instant award (such as a £5 pen) whenever someone submits a reasonable suggestion, perhaps followed by a larger award if significant savings ensue. Once you have instituted high awards, you cannot revoke them.

A suggestion scheme works best if the accent is less on savings and more on effectiveness. One company's form says: 'Your idea is worth submitting if it will help achieve any of the following:

- save time, materials or money;
- reduce or avoid costs;
- improve levels of quality, reliability, availability or service;
- enhance standards of safety, health or security;
- increase production.'

Publicising the results of good suggestions can encourage more. When you have a credible suggestion scheme the people who take part in quality projects often use the suggestion outlet for other ideas as change begins to ferment in the organisation. A good suggestion scheme will have fast response and maximum openness. The people on the suggestion committee must be trusted; their minds and minutes must be open.

Suggestion schemes are often an indication of how involved and empowered people feel. The more outlets they have for their ideas on improving the work, the more likely they are to use the suggestion scheme as well. Thus, if you have quality teams, and regular two-way meetings, and group-generated performance data, you are likely to have a lively suggestion scheme too. However, if the scheme is too slow and judgement too ponderous, or seen to be unfair, the scheme will dry up and good ideas will be lost.

Tannoy system The terrible Tannoy is not unlike those anxiety-inducing loudspeakers British Rail engineers specialize in producing for railway stations – loud enough to interrupt everything, and utterly inscrutable except for the one word that indicates the message would have been for you, if you had been able to make it out.

Some organisations have lovely ladies speaking in dulcet tones over well-tuned hi-fi loudspeakers – and they are *still* anxiety-inducers. I recognise that the Tannoy may seem convenient for calling people from a noisy factory floor to come and take a phone call, but a network of people willing to nip out and tell someone something must be better than bothering everyone in the name of 'efficiency'.

In a few benighted places management feels it must use the loudspeakers to explain or promote policy – a dreadful imposition on employees, who cannot even see the speaker. I second John Adair's advice: 'Drop your loudspeaker in a bucket of water at the earliest possible opportunity.'

Team briefing Specifically, team briefing is the name the Industrial Society has established for its form of top-down cascade communication, for management to keep employees informed. The monitoring structure for team briefing is sound, and often robust, but there is a serious tendency for top-down systems to silt-up with irrelevant or poorly edited material, no matter how much the initial sheep-dip training or written guidelines emphasised the manager's need to interpret the information at each level. People are too deferential (or afraid) to cut one precious word of the boss's golden prose. In some organisations the situation is so serious that the name 'team briefing' comes to stand for 'all the boring bumf', and any attempt to improve communication has to rest on whatever else people call the meetings where they talk about 'real' (that is to say, relevant) things. See 'Group meeting', 'Staff meeting', 'Team meeting', and Chapter 14.

Team meeting The primary purpose of work group meetings is to enable managers to manage. This is where a group can review:

- Progress (How do we know if we are winning?).
- Reasons why (decisions, variances, etc.).
- Impending events (we hear it first from our own boss).
- People – births, marriages and deaths.
- Checkpoint and feedback for staff queries.
- Action required (with reasons why).

The 'hear it first' aspect only works if managers are well informed.

Good meetings depend on good training. A few basic principles:

- Schedule for the year – publicise and stick to your schedule.
- Manage meeting time – open discussion but brisk pace.
- Chase answers for all queries people raise.

Team meeting notes Many work group meetings founder on either too little or too much structure. Instead of typed agendas or minutes it can be very useful for one member to take a few headings by hand, make a copy for the meeting record book, and post the original on the work-groups' wall. To underscore the fact that a single sheet, hand-written, is all that is wanted, a pre-printed form can be helpful.

Thank you People need to know how they are doing. In addition to formal appraisal they need (and deserve) informal feedback –

and 'Thank you' is the most effective (and inexpensive) form of informal feedback. Very few managers remember to use it. See 'Recognition' and 'Awards'.

Training refresher Most courses build close links among their members. Bringing participants back together regularly not only reinforces the training with shared experience, but also reinforces the informal links they use to communicate about other factors that can improve performance.

Video In large organisations not everyone can see the top brass doing whatever it is they do. Video can be useful in team meetings to give everyone the same brief message, which can then be discussed in the meeting. Video should always be brief and factual, and is best when people can focus on their own performance related to wider performance information.

Video can be dreadful! 'Shall we put the chairman on video – and show him on an endless loop in the canteen?' Resist the temptation!

Small screen should mean small group. Video can show senior people and events vividly, just as people are accustomed to seeing people and events on television at home. But at work it must not be unsupervised communication. The information should be introduced and presented by well-briefed supervisors, who can interpret what the video information means for their own groups. It helps if some of the people on the screen are us, real employees known to the watchers.

Walkabout Like doctors walking around wards checking on patient progress, senior managers need to walk around in the various areas of their subordinates, to check on staff progress. The purpose is not, 'How's your wife?' but:

- to ask about performance;
- to 'catch people doing things right';
- to make sure the communication that managers intend is perceived right through the system; and
- to make sure the communication that staff members want is also getting right through the system.

Walkabout can induce guilt in busy managers; it works well when the manager takes someone along to record questions raised, any promises made, and to follow up and get answers back to those who asked – and to communicate more widely as necessary. See 'Management by walking about' and 'Management by sitting in'.

The Pick-and-mix Survey

This is a collection of statements suitable for an employee attitude survey, from which you can select to suit yourself. Many topics are expressed here in slightly different ways. It is usually unnecessary (and expensive) to ask people the same thing too many times; they feel manipulated, and you gain no more wisdom than if you had asked only once. Just choose the version that suits you best.

Many organisations use an array of boxes after each statement:

Strongly agree	Agree	Disagree	Strongly disagree
□	□	□	□
□	□	□	□
□	□	□	□
□	□	□	□

Sometimes you can use a simpler format:

Agree	No opinion	Disagree
□	□	□
□	□	□

Some prefer to force a choice and leave out any neutral or no-opinion option; some people do use these responses to avoid being impolite or unkind. Whichever approach is used, consistent use of the same format will give perfectly valid and useful data, with clear comparisons between elements.

Most experts try to take the complex answers and simplify them for clear presentation. I would tend to combine 'Strongly agree' and 'Agree', and report back that '43 per cent agree' (compared with, say 49 per cent agreed in the next department, or the last year). Then you can graph the results, as shown in Chapter 17.

Most issues can be expressed in a positive or negative way. If a questionnaire is *too* positive people feel impelled to give the answers they think you want. A few issues (like 'too much paperwork') are simply too bland unless they are put in the negative. You can still graph the number who disagree, so you get a picture of the issue. Generally, employees are content with fairly positive wording, so long as they have the 'neutral' response through which to express violent disagreement. In the following list I have put the negative statements at the end of each section, to make calculation easy.

Empowerment

My views are fed into my organisation's strategies.
Most of my work methods are determined at my own location.
My boss is allowed to make decisions necessary to do our job well.
I am allowed to make decisions I feel are necessary to do my job well.
I can make changes to improve the way I do my work.
I am encouraged to find better ways of doing things.
I am involved in decisions that affect my work.
My team can make changes to improve the way we do our work.
I take part in setting my performance objectives.
I'm given real opportunities to improve my skills.
It's easy to make my views known to the right level of management.

I seldom worry that my job will change or disappear.
I seldom worry that my boss's job will change or disappear.
This division/unit is in control of its own future.
This division/unit has a clear sense of direction, clear goals, and strategies to achieve the goals.
My department has a clear sense of direction.
The lines of responsibility and authority in my department are clear.

Performance

I am quite clear what is expected of me in my job.
I get enough feedback to know how well I'm doing.
I enjoy my work.
Conditions here help me to be almost as productive as I could be.
I have most of the equipment and support I need to do my job.
I get the leadership and direction I need to do my job well.
My manager is good at planning and organising our work.
My manager thanks me when I've done well.
My manager gives me regular feedback on my performance.
I am quite clear what my department/unit is expected to achieve.
I know how my work contributes to the organisation's achievements.
I am proud of the work I do.
We have the organisation and talent to cope with any competitor.
I am satisfied with the recognition I receive for doing my job well.
I am regularly asked how to improve the quality of my work.
My team measures its performance against customer requirements.
My work gives me a strong sense of achievement.
Appraisal meetings with my manager are useful to me.
My most recent appraisal was about _____ months ago.
My last appraisal was fair and reasonable.

Teams

I know how well my team is doing.

My team knows how our work helps to meet the organisation's objectives.
Our top management is interested in our team's work.
We work together well as a team.
We co-operate to get the job done.
I feel valued by the other people in my work group.
Our supervisor/foreman/team leader keeps us informed.
As a team we are quite well managed.
The running of our group has improved in the last year.

Leadership

Senior management sincerely wants good relations.
Senior management is aware of the difficulties under which I work.
We see our top leader at least once a month.
We can rely on senior managers to do what they say they will do.
Our management is willing to sort out problems.
Overall, my department is quite well managed.
My boss's boss often visits us.
Our managers don't hold back good performers from promotion or good transfers.
We see our supervisor/team leader at least once a day.
My supervisor knows what's going on.
My supervisor usually tells us things before we hear them on the grapevine.
When I have a problem, my supervisor usually listens to me.
People are usually thanked for a job well done.
Senior managers are not concerned about the effects of their decisions on staff.

Communication

The organisation keeps me fairly well informed.
I usually believe what I'm told about the organisation.
The organisation tries to get people's views and thinking

The organisation usually tells me about major developments before I see them in the press or on television.

Changes in our work or environment are fully explained to us.

It is easy to make my views known to the right level of management.

We have good communication within the team.

We have good communication between teams.

My team holds information meetings at least once a month.

Management plans in time for regular team meetings.

We usually learn something new in our team meetings.

We usually get rapid answers to questions raised in our team meetings.

I am generally satisfied with internal communication in the organisation.

You can usually believe what you hear about the organisation from the unions.

I get most of my information about the organisation from:
- ☐ the grapevine
- ☐ my immediate boss
- ☐ team meetings
- ☐ the unions
- ☐ top management
- ☐ the house journal
- ☐ notice-boards
- ☐ videos
- ☐ external media
- ☐ other_____

I would like to know more about:
- ☐ the organisation's plans for the future
- ☐ what other departments do
- ☐ job security and prospects
- ☐ how customers see us
- ☐ policies and procedures
- ☐ training and development
- ☐ other_____

Trade union sources are often the first with important news about the organisation

The thing that would bring the greatest improvement in our communications would be _____.

Management only tell us what they want us to know.

Much of the information I receive is irrelevant to me.
I have more information than I can cope with on most matters.
I feel isolated from other parts of the organisation.

Networks

We hear about useful experience from other locations.
I meet people from other departments who share my interests.
The organisation encourages internal networking.
I can take time off to go to professional or special-interest
  meetings.

Customer Requirements

Score these from 4 for 'very important' to 0 for 'least important'.
Next, score how well the organisation meets customer requirements, from 4 for 'very good' to 0 for 'very bad'.

	Importance	*Meet needs?*
Efficient paperwork	_____	_____
Efficient and fast response	_____	_____
Courteous and helpful staff	_____	_____
Keeping to promised dates	_____	_____
Management available to customers	_____	_____
Smart, well-groomed staff	_____	_____
Clean offices or vehicles	_____	_____
Staff able to deal with problems	_____	_____
Fast response to emergencies	_____	_____

Training and Development

My job makes good use of my skills and abilities.
I am encouraged to tackle new problems.
I am satisfied with the training I've had for my present job.

I have a chance to get training for future jobs I might want.
My managers have given me good career guidance.
My manager is actively interested in my personal development.
I have a hand in planning my own training.
My boss and I use appraisals to help plan my training.

Culture

I'm happy with my working environment.
People here are willing to confront problems openly and solve
  them, rather than sweep them under the carpet.
Working here is no longer a job for life.
New technology always means loss of jobs.
Different departments work together well to get the job done.
Co-operation among departments is improving.
Most of the time it is safe to say what you think.
I believe information from this survey will be used to help the
  organisation improve.
There is too much paperwork in the system.
Personnel nowadays are more interested in procedures than
  people.
In our organisation you can get fired for _____.
In our organisation the way to get ahead is _____.
Our boss sometimes has to tell lies.

Open-ended

One thing to comment on in . . . is _____
One change to help me/us do a better job would be _____

Recommended Reading

Management research is at its best when it is based on observations of real life. A number of excellent people have done work that has slipped gently into my personal set of models. This cluster of models gains coherence and credibility as they work together seamlessly in real organisations. Other people have different assortments; valid work on how organisations work often overlaps, because human nature in all its variety contains some basic truths. Partly because of their style, these are my favourites.

Quite a few of them date back to the exhilarating climate of the 1960s and 1970s – what was it that liberated management thinking and sparked so much original work? Part of it was certainly the (American) combination of practical observation inside real organisations with opportunities for elegant theories to be appreciated. Perhaps MIT–Sloane played a part in creating a 'critical mass' of thinkers, striking sparks off each other.

The great Americans were peripatetic (like their ancient Greek models, moving about and moving the ideas with them); wherever they clustered they encouraged others. But it has been more difficult for the Europeans to gain the practice to combine with their theory; in European (and especially English) academic institutions consultancy is often regarded as 'not quite nice'.

Many of the more recent management books (including *In Search of Excellence* and its offspring) describe sensible implementations of these pioneering ideas. I think there is a need in Europe to create a new focus, as MIT did in the 1960s and 1970s, so that today's management thinkers can once again achieve critical mass and strike sparks off each other.

*   *   *

John Adair (1983), *Effective Leadership* (Aldershot: Gower) Adair's rather military model underlies much of the Industrial Society's work (and mine) on leadership and communication – three overlapped circles, distinguishing the different needs of the individual, the group, and the task. He sees the leader as managing the tension between the three. Adair's 1988 book *The Effective Communicator* gives an overview of team briefing in the context of other forms of management communication, with a useful section on report-writing.

Chris Argyris (1960) *Understanding Organizational Behaviour* (Boston: Dorsey) and (1964) *Integrating the Individual and the Organization* (New York: Wiley). Argyris came from the disciplines and language of psychology and education to look at motivation and how organisations can fuse individual personality into their formal needs. His concern with individual growth permeates all his work, and needs to be considered again for the 1990s.

R. Meredith Belbin (1981), *Management Teams* (Oxford: Butterworth-Heinemann). Belbin's work is the core of Chapter 3, a listing of eight different characters who make up an effective team. Many people have used Belbin's work in different ways, with differing degrees of sophistication. Mine is quite simple: a group exercise, putting results on a flip chart, which takes minimum time to get maximum sharing of information about group role preferences. For me, the idea is to use Belbin's model to help negotiate among team members to ensure that all the roles are consciously covered.

Warren Bennis (1975), *The Temporary Society*, and (1989), *On Becoming a Leader* (Reading, MA; Addison-Wesley). I chose these from among a number of major works from this eclectic American (with whom I enjoyed collaborating on a 1976 study of governance in American universities). These two encompass some of his most interesting ideas on leadership, groups, and how organisations work. Today we especially need to look again at non-bureaucratic ways of organising. Some of Bennis's thinking needs to be implemented more, including 'temporary systems'.

Per-Olof Berg (1978), *The Emotional Structures of Organisations* (Lund: Lund University). Berg's work (in English, from his thesis for Stanford Business School) was important to me as much for his method as his conclusions. He studied a Scandinavian glass company by identifying 63 dramatic events – 'Was that before or after the Personnel Manager was fired?' Berg distinguished in his interviews between 'key actors' and 'key observers,' which helps to explain why people are so often disappointed that the observer, who sees all, does nothing, and the actor, who does all, sees nothing. I believe Berg has caught the nature of the actors and observers, and it is we who demand too much from them who must change our expectations.

Robert Blake and Jane Mouton (1964), *The Managerial Grid* (New York: Gulf). This brought us the '9–1 manager', measuring people-focus and task-focus. Like Belbin's work, the Blake and Mouton grid was widely used, and helped people to look at their own styles and understand the limitations and expectations of others.

Wilfred Brown (1971), *Organization* (London: Heinemann). Lord Brown and Elliot Jacques did important work at Glacier Metals (where Lord Brown was the leader and Jacques the theorist), particularly looking at a manager's 'time span' of control. Do you decide 30-minute things, or five-year things? Of the two I chose to include Lord Brown here because it takes real courage to try to run a large organisation in accordance with theories about behaviour.

Eliza G. C. Collins (1984), *Dearest Amanda . . . advice from an executive to her daughter* (New York: Harper & Row). Liza Collins was senior editor at *Harvard Business Review* when she wrote this adept little book, which captures accurately the feelings as well as the situations women face in large organisations.

Russell Currie (1968), *Work Study* (London: Pitman for BIM). In this classic Gilbreth's and Taylor's thinking were updated for modern organisations. More than that, as a key manager at ICI, he identified and developed a generation of fine organisation development people – schooled with their stopwatches in work study techniques, but liberated beyond that to look for ways to improve the human side of the equation.

Peter Drucker (1988), 'Leadership: More Doing Than Dash', *Wall Street Journal*, 6 January 1988, and (1987), 'Personal View', *Strategic Planning Society News*, July/August 1987. These two small pieces are close to hand, but I still remember trying to review Drucker's 900-page 'bible', *Management*, in 1977 when I had to leave at six the next morning to catch a plane. The massive tome contained a wonderful seven-page chapter called 'On being the right size'. Drucker illustrates Adair's point that style is at least as important as content.

Paul Evans and Fernando Bartolome (1980), *Must Success Cost So Much?* (London: Grant McIntyre). These Insead professors interviewed wives as well as managers, to reach the conclusion that the people who reach the top do a better job of balancing and managing their home lives as well as their working lives. In today's frenetic climate, with too many overloaded and too few employed, personal balance needs to be valued more.

David W Ewing (1990), *Inside the Harvard Business School* (New York: Times Books/Random House). Ewing's career as Managing Editor of the *Harvard Business Review* gives him a unique view of the world's first great business school, inextricably linked with (and conceivably trapped in) the case study method of teaching. Ideas that are important today, like informal groups, participative management, and power-sharing came out of HBS in earlier times, often helped by David Ewing's deft editorial hand, eye and ear.

Pehr Gyllenhammar (1977), *People at Work* (Reading, Mass: Addison-Wesley). (I helped to bring this to fruition, so one can understand my bias in its favour.) In addition to describing the ideas behind what Gyllenhammar did at Volvo in the 1970s (including pioneer job-sharing, nearly autonomous group working, and bringing the stores to the work groups), this book raises such questions as why we should have an eight hour working day. Computers are perfectly able to calculate pensions and benefits in smaller, more manageable units – and as computers continue to reduce workforces, we should revisit these ideas.

Charles Handy (1976), *Understanding Organisations* (London: Penguin). Every reading manager I know has a copy of this book (usually the Penguin edition, well thumbed) in his or her bookcase. Charles Handy combines the practical experience of marketing and personnel management inside Shell with being a professor at MIT–Sloane and the London Business School, not to mention the wider scope he has gained as Warden of St George's House, Windsor. I like his pictures of the future of work (1984); I do not, however, think they will come true through corporate planning, but individuals with fax machines and PCs can already take ownership of their own diaries to make the 'tele-cottage' a reality.

Michael Beer, R. A. Eisenstat and Bert Spector (1990), 'Why Change Programs Don't Produce Change', *Harvard Business Review*, November-December 1990. A landmark study by three Harvard Business School professors. Once again, good observation is certainly the key to good management theory. Their work showed how middle-outward 'task alignment' in large organisations is more likely to work than top-down 'programmatic change'. Their 1990 book is called *The Critical Path to Corporate Renewal* (Cambridge, Mass.: Harvard Business School Press).

Fred Herzberg (1966), *Work and the Nature of Man* (New York: World Publishing). Herzberg's work on hygiene factors and motivators was so important in its time that we have rather come to take it for granted. (It was from Herzberg that I learned the consultant's trick of setting up a row of models, like 'Aunt Sally' targets, then demolishing all but one's own.) Pay is still a hygiene factor; gaining power is a motivator.

Malcolm Hillyard (1992), *Total Quality Management: Characteristics of Successful Programmes* (London: A. T. Kearney). This survey of large companies that had launched TQM programmes showed why they do not work. The few that do have clear, practical, measurable expectations, and ownership from the top. Quality concepts are important – perhaps Hillyard's clear, competent work can help keep them workable.

Geert Hofstede (1967), *The Game of Budget Control* (New York: Van Nostrand). This is the classic that shows how a 'negotiated' budget, where a manager has a chance to influence the process, will be met better than an imposed budget, where the subject has little voice. It fits everything I know about human nature in organisations, and in 1993 large organisations are still 'pushing down budgets' without giving people a chance to clarify their own realities and take part in the process. Hofstede did some brilliant work on the earliest employee attitude survey techniques inside IBM in the 1960s; from that work he was well armed to develop profiles of national characteristics, based on hundreds of thousands of responses from not-quite-look-alike IBM employees in 132 countries, in his 1980 book *Culture's Consequences* (London: Sage). I feel absolved of guilt when I write about national characteristics, so long as I stick to Hofstede's findings.

Rensis Likert (1961), *New Patterns of Management* (New York: McGraw-Hill). Likert's work inside organisations led to his thinking on motivation and management style, which in turn influenced many later theory-builders. It was he who first heralded the communication gap in hierarchies: about twice as many managers say they tell subordinates in advance about changes that will affect them, compared with the number of subordinates who say their managers tell them.

Michael Maccoby (1979), *The Gamesman* (New York: Simon & Schuster), and (1981) *The Leader*. In the latter book Maccoby studied six successful leaders in some depth. They were all intelligent, ambitious, pragmatic, good communicators, working by consensus rather than control. From very different viewpoints, they had all come to a similar point, where they felt critical of authority, and had to work out for themselves a *raison d'être* for their organisations. *The Gamesman* was even more important to me. Many people have developed 'taxonomies' or lists of types of managers, but I recognised all the members of Maccoby's list: the jungle fighter, the craftsman, the company man, the gamesman. And I felt better able to cope with them – especially the craftsmen, who still live in large organisations in large numbers, and truly care about what happens.

Abraham Maslow (1954), *Motivation and Personality* (New York:

Harper & Row). Maslow was the granddaddy of management theorists, and his work still underpins the latest in management thinking.

Elton Mayo (1945), *The Social Problems of an Industrial Civilization* (Cambridge, MA: Harvard). Mayo built on the Hawthorne studies and reached some important conclusions:
- People are motivated by social needs.
- Rationalising work has driven the meaning out of it, so people have to find meaning in relationships with their peers at work.
- The work group's values will influence behaviour more than incentives or controls from managers.
- Supervisors are effective only to the extent they can fill the social needs of their people.

D. C. McClelland (1961), *The Achieving Society* (New York: Van Nostrand). Remember 'N-Ach'? McClelland's work identified human needs (and thus motivations) in three categories: need for affiliation, need for power, need for achievement. Most people have some needs in each of these categories, but can be characterised (and managed) according to the strongest needs.

Douglas McGregor (1960), *The Human Side of Enterprise* (New York: McGraw-Hill). Father of 'Theory X and Theory Y', McGregor's work was based on fine observation inside American companies. Theory X management assumes that people are by nature lazy, supine, self-centred, stupid, gullible, and resistant to change. Theory Y sees people as motivated by goals and opportunities for development – and the job of the manager to take away the things that stop them from doing good work.

Henry Mintzberg (1973), *The Nature of Managerial Work* (New York: Harper & Row). This landmark study of what managers really do was Mintzberg's doctoral thesis, and formed a sound basis for his 1979 work, *The Structuring of Organizations* (Englewood Cliffs, NJ: Prentice-Hall). Mintzberg configures organisations on the basis of five basic parts: operating core, strategic apex, middle line, technostructure, and support staff. These are fed by five flows: formal authority, regulated information, informal communication, work constellations, and *ad hoc* decision-making. Co-ordination comes from another five: direct supervision, mutual adjustment, standardisation, output, and skills. A 5×5×5 cube that can be used to describe or prescribe for any organisation.

R. T. Pascale and A. G. Athos (1982), *The Art of Japanese Management* (Harmondsworth: Penguin). Pascale first brought to my attention the way the Japanese quietly manage the shift from 'what is claimed' to 'what is' – and the extended process they use for generating a widely-shared definition of a problem, which naturally leads to more rapid and conflict-free implementation of solutions.

Tom Peters and R. H. Waterman (1982), *In Search of Excellence* (New York: Harper & Row). Though some of their models (and mine, including IBM) have suffered since *Excellence* came out, the underlying observations were sound, particularly the emphasis on listening to customers. The breadth of their acceptance has been very heartening. There was a period where every manager at Ford was swotting up *Excellence* P. & W., though many organisations never made the real changes that should follow such top-management commitment.

R. G. Revans (1975), *Action Learning* (Harlow: Longman). Reg Revans has been in full revolt against the educational establishment, which must make it galling to see how deeply his ideas have infused formal education. In the classic action-learning model half a dozen managers exchange jobs, problems, organisations, and bosses, meeting each other regularly with a facilitator for co-consulting as they try to implement solutions to the complex problems. It is wonderful, and it works. Problems are solved and managers are developed.

E. F. Schumacher (1973), *Small is Beautiful* (London: Blond & Briggs). We all hark to Dr Schumacher's work, but it needs regular revisiting. It is his thesis that our difficulties and dangers come not from our failures but our successes – humankind is being distorted by the worship of economic growth. The book was written 20 years ago – an exciting time indeed! The only people who seem to have heeded it are the little enterprise companies that actually try to help people extruded from giant organisations start small ones.

Derek Sheane (1976), *Beyond Bureaucracy: the future shape and transformation of large complex organisations* (Bolton, Lancs: Management Research). Derek Sheane is known among ICI managers as one of the wilier change agents to emerge from the 1960s when Russell Currie was creating the concept and using it to help change this giant company. Derek's ability to foresee a federation of smaller organisations preceded and probably helped pave the way for John Harvey Jones, who injected into ICI the picture of a lean 'core' and a wide network of contractors. Sheane's little book concludes: 'I have come to prefer bottom-up visions: the type we build through dialogue in local situations, for in a complex interdependent society, central or top-down visions could only be tyrannous . . . we need to do it piecemeal, working out of local situations'.

Rosemary Stewart (1970), *The Reality of Management*, through to (1983) *Choices for the Manager* (Maidenhead: McGraw-Hill). Rosemary Stewart (like Derek Sheane) was able to work firsthand with large numbers of ICI managers, which gave rise to a series of excellent books about what managers really do, and the choices available to them in real and complex situations.

Valerie Stewart (1990), *The David Solution*, (Aldershot: Gower). Subtitled 'How to reclaim power and liberate your organisation', this book uses Valerie's extensive experience, including a good deal of consultancy inside British Rail, to help organisations free themselves from the lumps of marble in which they are encased (hence the title, which refers to Michelangelo's statue).

Robert Townsend (1970), *Up the Organization!* (London: Michael Joseph). One in the eye for ITT after Harold Geneen fired Townsend. Still valid, still naughty, still seen on many managers' shelves. Your most important PR person is the telephonist.

R. I. Tricker (1984), *Corporate Governance* (Aldershot: Gower). Bob Tricker was my boss at Oxford in the late 1970s, so I appreciate his skilful governance as well as his thinking. He believes that the concept of the company was a simple and successful device, rooted in nineteenth-century ideology. As companies became bigger, more concentrated, more diversified, more international, more complex, they diverged from their elegant, successful roots. He sees accountability at the heart of giving new life to subsidiaries, and new heart to the board's role.

Eric Trist (1960), *Socio-Technical Systems*, and (1963) *Organisational Choice* (London: Tavistock Institute). Trist's work, based on firsthand experience in the post-war coal industry, underpins much of the pioneering that went on in Scandinavian companies in the 1970s. The proof of the pudding is in Volvo's Kalmar factory, not the dissertations.

Peter Wickens (1987), *The Road to Nissan: Flexibility, Quality, Teamwork* (Basingstoke: Macmillan). Peter Wickens is Director of Personnel for Nissan in the UK, bringing to the Japanese considerable experience from Ford and others. My copy of his book has circulated more than any other management book I own – people at every level find in it pictures of a world to which they can relate. I suppose my strongest impression is the five-minute morning meeting – if Nissan can do it . . .

Index